Shyness

Become Extrovert, Confident And Overcome Shyness

(Techniques To Overcome Stress, Achieve Self Esteem And Succeed As An Introvert)

Martin Butler

Published By **Andrew Zen**

Martin Butler

All Rights Reserved

Shyness: Become Extrovert, Confident And Overcome Shyness (Techniques To Overcome Stress, Achieve Self Esteem And Succeed As An Introvert)

ISBN 978-1-77485-610-9

No part of this guidebook shall be reproduced in any form without permission in writing from the publisher except in the case of brief quotations embodied in critical articles or reviews.

Legal & Disclaimer

The information contained in this ebook is not designed to replace or take the place of any form of medicine or professional medical advice. The information in this ebook has been provided for educational & entertainment purposes only.

The information contained in this book has been compiled from sources deemed reliable, and it is accurate to the best of the Author's knowledge; however, the Author cannot guarantee its accuracy and validity and cannot be held liable for any errors or omissions. Changes are periodically made to this book. You must consult your doctor or get professional medical advice before using any of the suggested remedies, techniques, or information in this book.

Upon using the information contained in this book, you agree to hold harmless the Author from and against any damages, costs, and expenses, including any legal fees potentially resulting from the application of any of the information provided by this guide. This disclaimer applies to any damages or injury caused by the use and application, whether directly or indirectly, of any advice or information presented, whether for breach of contract, tort, negligence, personal injury, criminal intent, or under any other cause of action.

You agree to accept all risks of using the information presented inside this book. You need to consult a professional medical practitioner in order to ensure you are both able and healthy enough to participate in this program.

Table of contents

Chapter 1: Understanding Social Anxiety Issues.. 1

Chapter 2: Shyness And Problems 6

Chapter 3: Professional Intervention And Shyness 13

Chapter 4: Building Your Resistance 18

Chapter 5: Causes Of Shyness 22

Chapter 6: Cognitive Behavioral Therapy 26

Chapter 7: General Information 32

Chapter 8: Facing Society 40

Chapter 9: Social Phobias Or Shyness 44

Chapter 10: Understanding The Underlying Reason 56

Chapter 11: Heredity Or Our Genes 63

Chapter 12: Meeting New People 84

Chapter 13: Shake The Shyness - A Practical Guide 93

Chapter 14: Social Anxiety Support 98

Chapter 15: Acceptance And Commitment Therapy 103

Chapter 16: Managing Unhelpful Thoughts 108

Chapter 17: Shyness In Business 116

Chapter 18: Tips For Overcoming Your Shyness 125

Chapter 19: Top 10 Fears People Feel 141

Chapter 20: Preparation 147

Chapter 21: Your Workout Plan To Overcome Fear 152

Chapter 22: Your Mental Exercise Routine 157

Chapter 23: How Social Anxiety, Shyness, And Its Effects On Your Life 162

Chapter 24: Tips To Overcome Shyness 171

Conclusion 184

Chapter 1: Understanding Social Anxiety Issues

What is Social anxiety?

It's the fear that others will judge you if you have to meet strangers at a social event. An individual can feel crippled by this fear and avoid social gatherings that may cause embarrassment. It is more than being shy and nervous. This situation is most common at social events, where fear of being judged or ridiculed by others can be a problem.

These individuals know these emotions are unfounded and unnecessary, but struggle to overcome them. Although being judged in public and embarrassed is a common fear, each individual's personality may be different. The most common social phobia is the fear of giving speeches to an unknown audience or performing in front them.

It may seem impossible to cure such a disorder. However, there are ways around it.

What triggers Social Anxiety Disorder

This fear is most commonly triggered by the following situations:

Meeting unfamiliar people

Exams of any type

Interviews

Making presentations

Being supervised

Public speaking:

Stage performances

Meeting celebrities and other famous/authoritative persons

To speak out in a meeting

Making or receiving phone call

Criticism, or being teased

Going on a Date

Attend parties

Most of us feel the jitters whenever we meet an authority figure, a celebrity, or undertake a new assignment. Sometimes we feel shy and uncomfortable when we approach or converse with strangers. This cannot be considered social anxiety because it is a fleeting feeling that can be overcome by a little encouragement and guidance from others.

Although nervousness and shyness cannot be attributed to social anxieties, both these characteristics are part of the disorder. Social anxiety is when someone is constantly anxious. This feeling becomes a major obstacle in their day-to day functioning. This feeling eventually leads them to make excuses for not attending such events. Even if the men are strong enough to brave the occasion, they eventually give up and abandon it.

Shyness and social anxiety

Many people are confused about the differences between shyness and social anxiety disorder. Both are distinct. A personality trait called shyness, shyness does NOT have the negative emotions associated social anxiety disorder. Shy people live a normal life

Social anxiety disorder refers to a condition where the fear of or the quality of avoidance is constant for a longer duration, such as six months or more. It can be described as a substantial amount of fear of humiliation of chagrin that affects one to a particular extent. It makes him avoid situations or causes him to feel disquieted. A feeling of insecurity and the expectation that they will be rejected is another result. This feeling makes it more worried about what others will think.

This condition is called developmental and social anxiety. The majority of children are able to overcome this problem. But, if the condition persists or resurfaces it is called chronic social anxiety. Researchers are still trying to find the cause of this disorder. Another shocking fact is that not all socially anxious people have shyness and not all anxious people have shyness.

Chapter 2: Shyness and Problems

Where can shyness cause problems? Anytime. It can cause problems in your professional as well personal life. This can limit your potential to get the life you want. This is the reason shyness must be overcome.

Job market is one place where being shy can be a problem. It is likely that you will be competing with other applicants for a job. If you're not confident and aren't as self-deprecating as you could be, you might get overlooked while you search for employment.

Employers review hundreds of potential job candidates. While interviewing job seekers, each person blends with the other. If you have something you can stand out, you will be more likely to get the job. But if you don't have something that makes you stand out, it is less likely that you will be considered for the job. Naturally, if shyness is a problem, you will try to find a way that you won't stand out when applying for a position. This can lead to you being overlooked by potential employers, which can negatively impact your job search.

Many people believe that having the right qualifications on a resume is enough to get the job. They think their resume will sell them and get them the job. They are unaware that an interview is required to obtain the job. In some cases, more than one interview may be required to hire for a job. Someone who is shy could come off as being too timid in a job interview. This can lead to them not being hired for a job where they are highly qualified. Employers, who are human beings, tend to pick the people with whom they have the best relationships.

A lack of confidence is a sign that you don't want to be shy when applying for a job. People who find it difficult to speak with strangers and are uncomfortable around other people will have more difficulty in job interviews. They may need to interview for three more jobs before they get hired.

Personal life is also affected by your shyness. Shy people find it difficult to take advantage of all the opportunities they have to meet new people. If they don't have someone to hold them accountable, they will not go to social events. This means that they are often restricted in their friendships and in their activities.

A shy person is simply not able to enjoy the same benefits of someone who is not shy. They feel the same way if they have a handicap. Being shy in today's world is like having a nice car and no driver's license. You will not be able enjoy the same joys that others have, like meeting new people.

Dating is a difficult subject for shy people. They are more likely to choose someone they don't like over someone they care about. They may be unable to grow emotionally because they are glued to the same group of friends.

When young people are shy, they often find themselves in the "wrong crowd" when they enter Junior High and High School. They do this because they are afraid of not fitting in so they tend befriend people who are already friends. In an effort to feel accepted by others, they might resort to drinking, smoking or drug use. This can stop them from realizing their dreams and helping others when they are most needed.

This chapter's subtitle is "When shyness may be a problem." It can affect you as an adult, as well as your child. It can also impact your personal life and work life. It has a negative impact on every aspect your life.

It is possible to overcome shyness at any age by becoming aware of it and working on ways to overcome it. You must push yourself every day to break out from your comfort zone. This can be as simple and easy as saying "hello!" to a new person every single day. Shyness does not last forever. If you don't want to feel shy, then you don't have to be. This is something you can conquer.

Here are some tips to help you overcome your shyness

1. Volunteer

Volunteering your time for community causes or events will force you to engage with others on an interpersonal level. It is simple to find ways that you can help others and volunteer. This takes little time, but can make you more social and help you get out of your own comfort zone.

2. Talk to strangers

It is important to learn how to make small talk with strangers in places like the bank, grocery, and cleaners. It's easier to have conversations and meet new people when you start to talk to strangers. Conversations do not need to be deep. People can just chat about the weather and general topics. It will become second nature when you speak to people more often.

3. Join a Club

There are clubs available that cater to specific interests. You can search www.meetup.com in order to find clubs close by and help promote your interest. You don't need to be afraid to attend these clubs. A lot of people who attend them do so alone.

4. Take care yourself

Your confidence will increase if you feel confident about yourself. If you feel confident about your appearance, you will be more inclined to show it to others. When it comes to your appearance, take the time and care for yourself. You don't have have to be a movie star glamour to be confident. Only look your best.

5. Do not take it all personally

Fear is an important component of shyness. Fear of being rejected can be one of the main reasons people shy away. If you want your life to be successful, you have to overcome this fear. Don't believe that everything is about yourself. The chances are that the people you are speaking to have other thoughts than yours. There is something that makes a shy person or not shy different than someone who is more open to receiving feedback from others about how they see them. A shy person tends to think others are talking about or judging him/her, while a non-shy one is more likely to believe they aren't as concerned with them. Stop being afraid of rejection and take it personally. This is the key to overcoming shyness.

You don't need to complete the five above steps immediately. You can take your time and break out of the mold you created.

Chapter 3: Professional Intervention and Shyness

Everybody experiences anxiety from time-to-time. Sometimes anxiety can result from stressful situations such as meeting tight deadlines or social obligations. Mild anxiety in "small doses" can help you to be more focused and alert when facing difficult or threatening circumstances. Some people will eventually become shy if they've experienced fear and extreme anxiety that don't go away. A person may experience extreme shyness that interferes with their daily lives. It is possible to get treatment for this problem.

There are many forms of anxiety or shyness.

Each type of dog has its own distinct characteristics.

People who suffer from generalized shyness can have recurring concerns or fears. They might be concerned about their finances, or their current health. Others have a persistent fear that something bad will happen to their lives soon. In extreme cases these manifestations can make a person's life difficult.

Experts have suggested that fear and extreme shyness can result from insecurity and a misperception about one's potential. These feelings usually occur when there are not enough reinforcements from the society, family and school.

Post-traumatic stress disorder (PTSD), can occur in those who are suffering from severe emotional and/or physical trauma. This is closely tied to anxiety and shyness. This can lead to changes in behaviour patterns, feelings, or thoughts. This may occur months or even decades after the event.

People who feel shy might be unable to pinpoint the exact moment they will feel panic attack. People with shyness may restrict their activities to stop fear from taking over.

Many psychological disorders are associated with extreme fear about certain objects and situations. These triggers will eventually make a shy person act if they are presented.

It is vital to address shyness.

If you do not address shyness, it can impact your quality and life. Avoidance behaviour can lead more problems such as conflicts with your job requirements, basic daily tasks, and family obligations. People who feel shy often also suffer from psychological disorders such as depression. This may lead to problems such as substance abuse. These people may have strained relationships and conflicts with family members, friends, or colleagues. You may also notice a decline in your school or work performance.

To overcome shyness, you can seek professional help.

Most cases involving shyness can be successfully managed by trained mental professionals. These professionals include licensed psychiatrists or psychologists. Cognitive behavioural Therapy (CBT), which has been proven effective in the treatment of shyness, was supported by research. CBT can be used by psychologists to help you recognize and eventually manage certain triggers.

This type is a behavioural therapy that uses techniques to curb or decrease shyness. You might learn to relax and practice deep breathing exercises. These will help you to counteract your shyness and other symptoms.

Cognitive therapy can help you learn how your thoughts can influence your shyness. These things can be changed by you to reduce the severity and frequency of your reactions to unfavorable factors. Your cognitive awareness is often combined with behavioral techniques. You can gradually confront and tolerate shyness-inducing circumstances in a safe and controlled environment.

In addition to psychotherapy, your professional may recommend the appropriate medication. This will allow you to have your case managed by many different treatment providers. This is crucial to ensure that your case will be treated holistically. You need to be aware that there may be side effects from the drug during treatment. Notify your doctor immediately if these side effects occur. This team will closely monitor the effects of any medication changes or modifications. This can help prevent unwanted reactions, such as excessive trembling/sweeping.

Chapter 4: Building your resistance

Now that your knowledge and understanding of why you feel shy around other people and in particular situations is better, it is time build your resistance to shyness.

The chapter 1 exercise will have prepared and prepared you for the next step. Working on your triggers is the best way to get comfortable with your shyness.

To make this activity even more fun, you need to engage and challenge. This chapter will be about training your mind, and building your resistance to situations when your shyness threatens you with silence.

1. Programming your mind

It is easy to become shy when you put yourself in situations where this happens. Try taking a backseat and observing what your body and mind are doing. A person's past experiences can influence how they react to certain situations. To overcome shyness, your mind must be programmed. This begins by questioning your reaction.

Ask yourself if feeling shy is a rational response. It is important to remember the importance and focus on the task at hand. Pay attention to what your mind says you should do. Is it telling you to stay silent or to move away, or to shine the spotlight on others? Try to push yourself beyond your comfort zone, and do exactly the opposite.

This reaction sets off the journey of retraining you mind and your reaction to situations where it is easy for you to become shy. You will be able to improve your confidence quickly if it is a difficult task.

2.Endurance Training

Your task to overcome your shyness should be considered a sporting event. You have now completed the phase of theory and comprehension. Now you must begin the physical training.

Endurance is training to overcome shyness. Reassess your trigger list. Choose a task which is likely to cause mild shyness. This should be something that is easily accessible for you. This could be as simple to say "Good morning" to colleagues, or to smile at passers-by.

After you've settled on the task, let yourself be exposed to the situation. Next, observe. Consider how long and how far you are able to endure the situation. This can be achieved in one or both of the following ways. You can increase the amount of exposure or engage in further discussions.

For instance, if one or two people can't smile at you on the way to work, smile at three or more people. This increases the likelihood of you feeling shy, which can lead to increased resistance.

On the other side, you can increase your engagement even further by making a point to speak with your colleague in the morning. This allows you to face your shyness and builds your confidence.

Chapter 5: Causes of Shyness

It is essential to be able to recognize your shyness in order to overcome it. You can't tell yourself to be more socially outgoing and expect that it will change you. It may be possible to have some effect with your willpower, but it won't change you.

Some people are born timid. If this is the case, then trying to overcome shyness can be likened to trying to make a mountain less steep with an axe. They cannot do anything except to learn coping skills to cope with social anxiety and introversion when in public.

There has to be something psychologically behind people who aren't naturally shy. If a child grew up being compared negatively to his brothers, he is more likely develop an inferiority Complex that manifests as shyness.

This chapter will focus on the causes of shyness and what you can do to overcome it.

Self-Confidence

Self-confidence and shyness are directly related. Lack of self-confidence is a sign that the brain attempts to protect someone by making them feel shy. Negative beliefs about your self can result in a lackluster self-confidence. It all boils down to what you think about yourself and how it is influenced by the world around. Even if they try hard to keep it from happening, constant negative feedback can have an adverse effect.

Complex of inferiority

Inferiority is a feeling that you are less than others. People with inferiority comp don't enjoy being reminded this fact. They may be more cautious and shy, as they are trying to avoid critics and other people. It can also indicate a reluctance for others to hear your ideas.

Perfectionism

If you are afraid of failure, and hate the feeling when things don't go as planned, you can give up. You may also experience a more serious form. Perfectionists tend to think that it's better just not to talk and do nothing than to try and say or do something wrong.

Social skills are lacking

If you don't understand how to make friends or have a conversation, you will likely feel awkward and scared. People develop social skills when they are young. Watching our parents interact with each other as children is a great example of how social interaction works. It is possible to lack social skills if you don't have the same people around you, or you find such things boring.

Past Trauma

It's not surprising that victims of trauma are more reserved than others and tend to prefer to keep things to themselves. Trauma is about people. In children's cases, this can mean a dysfunctional home, an abusive father, or a dysfunctional family. It could be bullying, identity-related attack, harassment, or abuse. This causes fear of people and society. As such, people are only safe when there are no other people around.

There may be more reasons, but these are major ones. We will be discussing how to overcome shyness in the following chapters.

Chapter 6: Cognitive Behavioral Therapy

Cognitive behavioral treatment is one way to deal with social anxiety disorder. However, it is not necessary to visit a professional to obtain this help. Instead, we will discuss the many aspects of this and how it can benefit you.

Cognitive behavioral therapy is at its core a method that helps people control anxiety by relaxing and breathing. We'll discuss their significance and explain why.

So what is it?

It's basically a type a talk therapy. It involves attending a few sessions. These sessions will help you become more aware that you can have negative, inaccurate, or poor thinking. It can be helpful for those with anxiety disorders, depression, PTSD, or eating disorders. It can also be used in stressful situations.

CBT has a unique advantage: you don't have to treat mental disorders with it. Instead, you can use it to improve your life.

While it does indeed help with depression and with anxiety, it can also help you to grow as an individual and treat many other conditions.

Thoughts are power

CBT places a strong emphasis on the fact that your perceptions, thoughts, or other factors are the sole influence of your behavior. One example is that if you feel stressed out, your perceptions of reality could be distorted. This is a belief that when you have your thoughts in line and understand the reality of what is happening, you will be happier. It also means that you will be able assess these thoughts more effectively and in a more positive way.

What does that have do with social anxiety, then? Anxiety refers to an irrational fear. However, social anxiety can be defined as the irrational belief people are against you. CBT is a way to assess your thoughts, those that lead you towards making harmful choices. It's the idea of creating a more rewarding and positive foundation for yourself that will allow you to have a better outlook and live a better lifestyle.

This is a good thing, as it provides anxiety sufferers with a clear picture of the reality. Reality can be hard and difficult to face. It can also be hard to be objective and see things accurately. The beauty of CBT, however, is the ability to create a better and more realistic reality.

CBT sessions can be very helpful if you think people are bad, for example, because of a past relationship with your parents. Maybe you hold onto the past and it's preventing you from moving on. Maybe you're aware that you may have problems, and need to fix them. Whatever the case, this helps you understand what the reality is and how you can overcome them.

Social Anxiety Parts

CBT can be used to help you see the root of your problem and then how to deal with it. We'll talk about the essential elements of CBT. And how you can use them.

The best part about CBT is that, while you can see a therapist online, or offline, you will also learn critical skills that you can apply to your own life.

We will discuss the key components of CBT and how it can help those with anxiety-related disorders.

We begin with an assessment. Here you'll be able to analyse and then identify which situations cause anxiety. The goal is to "learn your triggers" if you don't have a better expression. This is important because you need to know what drives you, and what makes your anxious.

After that, cognitive restructuring will be your next step. This is when you learn to recognize the thoughts that are causing social anxiety. What is it that causes you to feel this? In essence, you'll look at them, and discover the real logic behind them. It's not easy because you might believe that your idea for using it is quite rational. The reality is that it's not. If you continue to hold on to negative thoughts, you will make yourself unhappy. Let's restructure the situation and find out the truth.

This is mindfulness training. This basically means that you can learn to stay present and not be distracted by regrets from the past or negative interpretations about the future. We'll get into this more in the next section.

Finally, once you feel comfortable with this, you can begin to reduce your anxiety by placing yourself in the situations that make you anxious. Then, you can use the bot cognitive skills we discussed in restructuring to increase mindfulness and decrease anxiety. This is basically what you do. You might be asking yourself why this is so. This is because you don't have to sit around and think about how to solve these problems. It will allow to you to become comfortable with these situations. By applying what you've learned, you'll find that you don't have to be so scared. It's not quite as scary as it seems. Social anxiety is something you create in your head.

The last step is to determine what you will do to get better. It's not always easy. It isn't easy. But it is possible for anyone to overcome this problem and make use of this opportunity to their advantage. CBT focuses on helping people overcome difficulties. You'll feel more in control of your negative thoughts. This will result in you feeling happier. The program lasts thirty days and will allow you to overcome your negative thoughts. In turn, this will lead you to a happier life. This is the key component of this program. We'll be more specific later.

Chapter 7: General Information

These tips won't work as well as they claim. They will not work long-term and can't help with dealing with public situations. Even though you can force yourself into talking to people, it won't help your low self-esteem, inferiority, or trauma. These issues need to be addressed if long-term solutions are possible. In the next chapter we'll discuss these issues.

Minor achievements

It's not the ultimate prize of the race; it's the little trophies, incentives and gratifications you get along the route that are important. Everyone will eventually arrive at their destination tomorrow or today. If you do not enjoy the journey, the race is over.

Small achievements could be those bizarre or strange pleasures that lead to something useful about life. Here is a brief illustration to help you understand this concept better.

Imagine you are preparing to present a presentation. You hyperventilate, so you turn to a book for calm. It could be anything you find distracting. It could be either a novel or an assortment of poems. Reading a book does not serve as your ultimate goal. It's merely a means to present your work professionally. However, you do end up learning from it.

This is the way you can make minor achievements and still achieve a great deal. Enjoying the little things in life can make it easier. Sometimes the race is more important than winning. Be aware that the end goal is not the only reason for a path. You should be able to smell the flowers and breathe the freshness of the air while you walk, and not only worry about being the fastest.

Stop Self-Criticism

Self-criticism can't be attributed to you being unhappy with yourself. It is caused by society being unhappy with them. The only role you can play in all this is that as a message-passer, you just pass it on to your mind and take it with you. According to the saying, man is his best critic. You can achieve success by critiquing and studying your behavior. Negative criticism can result from self-criticism. This could result in a substantial drop in self-esteem.

A great way to boost self-esteem is to get rid of your inner-critic by replacing him with an active, helpful voice. It's very simple to do this. Take control of your mind. If you notice a negative thought creeping in, speak up mentally and stop it. It can be helpful to repeat the phrase, "no this is not true, I am stronger than this," when negative thoughts are creeping into your mind.

Motivation

Motivation is vital for human success. Once you are able get rid of your inner critics, it is now time to replace them with motivation. Take a look at all the things that drive you, and create a list. These could be as simple and as important as a better physique or as significant as children or family. These are the steps you can take to make yourself more efficient:

If you feel down, remind your self of the benefits of confidence and why you are doing it. These positive thoughts, motives and ideas can be written out on large paper and posted around the house.

You should be able to concentrate on what you like instead of worrying about what you don't. The best way to feel confident is to get rid of all the negative things in your life. It is easy to feel motivated when you are passionate about something. Your inner voice is your guide when you are struggling to find the right thing in your life. You can ask your inner voice for help if you are feeling lost or confused. Then, ask your self what your goals should be and a rush of motivation will flood your mind.

Motivation can be addictive. Soon, you will develop a habit for thinking of ideas.

Talk to strangers

Even talking to acquaintances can seem intimidating for those who are socially awkward. It is important to talk with at least five strangers daily. Don't be alarmed if someone doesn't want to talk to you. Not all people are comfortable talking with strangers. You'll eventually meet people who are eager to chat with you, and maybe even make friends.

Talking with strangers offers many benefits. Talking to strangers will not only increase your self-esteem and confidence, but can also improve your attitude towards people. You will learn that first impressions are temporary and that people don't always look the same. You will also be able meet new friends and make new friendships.

Take care though. The primary purpose of this challenge, to boost your confidence, is to speak to strangers. Do not join any meeting or club that is specifically designed to meet new people. You can chat up strangers at any place, including malls.

Talking to strangers will boost your confidence in a number of ways. They won't judge or criticize you. Even if they did, their opinions are irrelevant. Even if it's embarrassing for you in front, it is possible they won't ever see you again.

Stop Comparing

Comparing yourself with other people is often seen as a way to get better at yourself and to help you be more competitive. However, it is easy to become complacent and destructive when you start comparing yourself with others.

Comparing yourself with others can lead to a never ending race for victory. A race in which mental and bodily health is sacrificed. The world is vast and everyone is capable of doing something better than you. Don't compare yourself with other people. Compare and compete with your own self. Compare your current self with the past to see how far your self-improvement has taken you. Pay attention to yourself and don't forget about others. Instead of getting jealous of others' successes or feeling happy about their failures, you should focus on your own achievements. This will make it difficult to build self-esteem.

Positivity

Try new things every single day, and get out of your comfort zones. It's normal to make mistakes and fall short at the beginning. This is normal. It is rare that anyone in the world ever learns something from their first attempt. People remember only the achievements and not the challenges that a person went through to make it to the top.

Try New Things

To keep yourself interested and motivated, it is important to challenge yourself daily to try new things. This will increase your confidence and help you stay alert. If you are willing to challenge yourself, you can step out of the comfort zone. This is a great way to boost self-esteem.

It does not have to be something remarkable or spectacular every day. You can do something more than sitting back and slacking. It will bring life to your life and help you appreciate yourself.

It does not have to be a goal. However, it is important that these activities lead to self-confidence.

Don't force yourself into an activity if it is too daunting or difficult. Do something you find easy. When you are more relaxed, you can always return back to the previous activity.

Chapter 8: Facing Society

Get prepared to tackle these situations head-on. Sometimes you may feel like there is no way to communicate with others or that you don't know where to start. If that is the case then you should take some time to prepare. Research fashion, food, sports and any other topics you find your friends discussing. No one has to be impressed. It is enough to have a conversation.

The conversations can be broken down into phases. Phase one starts with the "hi" phrase and then moves on to phase 2, which is the introductions or renewals of conversations. Phase three can be difficult. Browse through the many topics you have in common. Phase four: The departure. You could exchange numbers and emails, as well as cards. Mention how much you enjoyed talking to them.

Make little comments and add phrases to what you say. This will reduce awkward answers of one word. Do not say "That blazer really suits your style", unless someone says so. Instead, respond with "Thanks!" Red is my lucky colors." This brief phrase opens up a world of possibilities as to what next. Your acquaintance could choose either to discuss Red or Luck. Look at how you helped him choose his next move.

Another way to start a conversation is with the "have any of you ever tried ...."? Line." Let's assume you're a passenger on the bus, and you see someone you kind-of knows. You could also say, "Have they ever made the latte over there?" It's one of the best I ever had."

Here's an easy trick you can use to celebrate something while you're out and about. You may not be familiar with many people. You can approach smiling people, which is the opposite of intimidating, and strike up a conversation. You can start by saying "Haven't seen your around before" or "Having fun?" I'm ..." once you have gotten the hang of it, speak up and talk to more people. Once you are able to establish a rhythm, your confidence levels will soar. It's not necessary to strike up deep conversations with these people. Just move on to the next person. This will make it so your nerves don't get the best of you.

Remember to be aware of how your posture reflects on you. As you begin to talk to someone, think back to how you used stand when you were younger. It's also a good idea to pay attention to other peoples' body language and postures. Do they seem closed-off or are they discussing something private? Perhaps this isn't the best time for you to approach them. Don't be afraid to take the advice and move on. Mary could be telling Jane the story about her boyfriend breaking up with her. This is not to say they don't like you. It's just that it's not a good time for chat.

Keep a smile on face. People will see you as friendly and approachable if you smile. In all cases, you should maintain a steady and relaxed breathing. This will calm the mind and body.

It doesn't matter how many times you practice with yourself in the mirror or with others. You'll be fine and will get over shyness quickly. If you find yourself in adverse situations, which there will always be, you'll be better equipped for them. There will always exist people who make you feel terrible about yourself. It is best to avoid these people.

Chapter 9: Social Phobias or Shyness

We talked in the previous chapters about shyness, and how it often starts in the lives of shy people. In the preceding chapter, we covered shyness as an overall condition and its impact on individuals. We'll be looking at shyness in greater detail.

Shyness, Social Phobia

I've mentioned before that there is a variety of levels of shyness. What you experience will determine if it is shyness, Social Phobia, or Selective Museum.

First of all, shyness can be a sign that you are not suffering from a mental illness. In modern society, people want to be able to diagnose every condition as a mental illness and order medication or electric shock therapy. It is easier to treat symptoms than find a cure. We have become a society where we just take the pills and hope it makes us feel better. Instead of actually talking to someone to learn the truth and find the solution, we are too busy rushing to get the cure. Symptoms vs. cure.

Let me just mention two forms. The first form is general shyness.

Shyness

As we have said, shyness will eventually go away. Shyness refers to a condition in which you are uncertain about a situation. Once your comfort zone is established, you will feel okay.

Social Phobia

Social Phobia, an extreme form of shyness, is called "Social Phobia". If someone is suffering from social phobia, they will do anything to get out a social situation. They will find a way around going to work or attending a social event like a party. If they can't get up the courage to do these things then they will find an excuse to not go.

Social phobia means that someone with panic attacks, terrors sweats, or freeze ups can occur. The severity of the attack will determine if they are able to black out or not.

Social Phobia can lead to someone becoming a recluse and hermit. They will have very little contact with the outside world and, if they do, it'll be on their terms and in a way planned for them.

For instance, if they have to get to the store at night, they may go first thing in morning. The store will not allow for much social interaction. They will have a list or a plan that shows where all the items are located in the store. They will make a plan for their time in the stores.

Shyness. Social Phobia. Stage Fright.

In this example, we will be talking about the difference between shyness, socialphobia, and Stage Fright. Like I mentioned before, shyness can be characterized as a fear of social situations. Stage Fright is a condition which allows you to interact with people on a larger scale.

Stage fright can be described as a situation in which you must deal with many people and make yourself known to the world. Stage fright is the fear that someone will put themselves out there to entertain and give of their own self. Stage fright happens when someone performs before a group. It can be five people, ten persons or thousands.

Stage Fright is not a rare condition. Stage Fright can be experienced by anyone who has ever tried to judge or give their best through a performance or play.

When I was in Middle School, Santa Clause was my role in a school play. We were doing a reenactment to Alvin & the Chipmunks Christmas story. This is for anyone who doesn't recall where Alvin finds the golden harmonica. It ends up saving a child. You must watch this video if it hasn't been seen before.

Anyway, the play was reworked and I was cast as Sana Clause. I was dressed up and sat on a stool reading the story to them. Even worse, the day before my big performance, I became sick and took 103 degrees.

From my memory, I only remember being thirteen. I was in middleschool which was between 5th and 7th grades. I didn't know what I was doing, I was nervous to do the show in front of everyone and I was even more sick than a dog. But I knew I had the strength to perform so I brought three thermoses full of chicken soup with me and went out.

It was one the best things I've ever done. I was scared and sick but I knew that this was something that I needed in order to develop my personal character. Looking back now at that time I wonder how my future would have turned. I might have thought about that moment for years, but I didn't make the best decisions in my life. You might have made different decisions or made different choices. If so, you wouldn't be living your life now.

You're right, it was a stupid school production. Yes, it was correct. While I'm certain that most people didn't know it or thought about it for more than 30 years, the fact I am now talking about it to them in this story is proof that it was important in my life.

The decisions you make in your daily life will determine the direction of your life. You might also think that this is going to be too much thought and insight to write an ebook. However, take a step back and examine your life. Take a moment to reflect on all the events in your past and consider how they may have influenced your life.

It really makes one think.

Stage fright and other social events can make a big difference in your life. Every decision you make will affect your confidence, your character, and the way that the world sees and perceives you.

The Foundation for A Social Phobia

Social phobias don't happen overnight. It is a gradual and progressive condition. It begins with minor things, like stage fright, fear or rejection, or social embarrassment. If these actions do not change, they will start to form a pattern. If you reject an invitation to a party for the third time, then another, then another, then even another, then you should ask yourself why.

Is it because you're not comfortable with your friends? What if you have a hard time getting to work at the proper hours? What is the problem?

I like to use movies as a reference in many of my books. It allows people with an interest in the subject to view the movie through my eyes. This allows them to take away my views and also form their own opinions.

Jim Carrey stars in "Yes Man" as the main character. This movie is a great example of shyness and I encourage you to watch it. Jim Carrey plays Jim Carrey's main character. He avoids all social interaction except with his friends. You see him at the beginning of the movie going to the video shop to rent a DVD.

Jim Carrey calls his friend just a moment later, and he refuses to answer until he finally does.

During this brief conversation, he lies to his friend about his home and says he is not. His friend sees his face through the window at the video store. He convinces him to go to the bar.

They all get down to the bar and start talking to one another. Jim Carries friend tells Jim Carries that he's having a bachelors party in one week and that he would like him to attend. Jim tells his friend that he is busy the night before and that he didn't tell him when it was happening. Jim establishes a negative social behavior that can be interpreted by the audience as shyness and/or social phobia. We don't know at this time why he doesn't want go to the party. However, in the next scene, we discover.

Jim sees the ex-girlfriend of his in the next scene. She is out and about with her new boyfriend. Jim is trying to leave the situation as he is shy, or embarrassed to see outside the relationship. Soon, a awkward situation emerges. Jim makes a comment then leaves the bar.

The Next day

Jim can be found at his bank job next day. He has proven himself to be intelligent and able to manage his environment. He is in an area that he can both control and work with others. He is surrounded in people who he regards as inferior. Norman, Norman's boss, is very social. Jim's boss Norman is quite the opposite. Norm enjoys hosting parties and other social events. Jim often refuses to attend.

Jumping a little further into the movie, Jim is seen outside enjoying his lunch. This is where you can still see that he's a socially isolated person. He shouldn't go out to eat in a restaurant, or at least eat in the bank. Because of his shyness or social anxiety, he chooses a comfortable place to sit. In this scene, we meet another character who was part of Jim's childhood. He approaches Jim to talk about all his adventures. He tells his friend that he has climbed mountains, wrestled wild animals, and many other unusual events that most people wouldn't consider doing in their lifetimes.

Jim's friend reveals to him that he was able to learn all this from the "Yes" Seminar. In this seminar, you're taught to say yes to life and all of the opportunities it presents, no matter how insane or bizarre they may seem.

Jim agrees at this point to attend the seminar. There you can see him looking at all those who showed up and then avoiding them. This is him displaying his social anxiety. Jim feels uncomfortable because he is seated next to a friend.

Here we reach the point where you are able to look back on your life and say "This moment in my life is where everything changes." Jim confronts fear and decides to take control of his life, changing the course of his future. As I looked back over my life and saw events that have shaped who I am, so does the rest.

The seminar begins from this point. Jim is named in the crowd the only NEW member. He replies, "Auditing", when asked if his participation is possible. The speaker tells Jim that it is impossible to audit life. He makes a vow with Jim to accept any opportunity that presents itself. Jim, an extremely impressionable person, now takes this literally and begins saying "YES!" for every event.

If you haven't already, I will let it be. I'll be honest and tell you that he gets into some bizarre situations and manages to escape them in Jim Carrey-style.

Jim wins the girl and has gained the confidence to fight for it. It was that one moment that changed Jim's outlook on his life and transformed his outlook.

It is important to examine your life with someone with fear or who suffers from shyness. It will be difficult, but you have to do it in your quest to make yourself a better individual.

We will be covering the next few chapters how to conquer shyness, social anxieties, anxieties, as well as other conditions that can impact your life.

We only have one chance at life. There are many people out there who don't like me. I don't even like them. I don't let that stop I from being the person and doing what it is I love. I am going the next chapter to build your confidence, get you ready for your fears, and help you restructure your life to make it the best it can.

I hope this chapter has helped you. Please go to the movie. It's a good movie for someone shy or suffering from social anxiety.

Chapter 10: Understanding the Underlying Reason

Ever wondered where shyness originated? You may have wondered, or maybe not. Not necessarily that you feel ashamed or lack confidence in yourself. But it's not. There are many introverts that have rich social lives.

Shyness means something different. What this really means is that your attention is always on you. Where is this discomfort coming from? If you can pinpoint the source of your discomfort, you will have solved a significant part of the problem.

Research has indicated that different sources could be possible depending on the situation. Not because your problem isn't unique. Because you are unique. Let's see what these options are, one by one. You can then determine if any of them resonate with your needs. Once you identify the root issue, it is one step closer in conquering it.

You can focus too heavily on your image and become anxious about how your face looks, how your talk, how your smile moves, what your face says when you smile and other tiny thoughts that swirl inside your mind. This anxiety can make you second-guess every step. You are too busy trying to be perfect that you don't come across as sub-par that you start to feel self-conscious. The problem lies in your belief that others are as attentive to you as you are to yourself.

As a child, you were stereotyped and labelled shy. Over the years, however, this has become a part of your personality. When we were young, we love our own company better than the others. But, being quiet does no mean that you should be shy. Perhaps you were a quiet, independent child who liked to play with one's toys more than the toys of others. This trait from childhood has stuck and you have been called "shy" by others. Intuitively, it feels like you have to live up and be true to yourself. But it could be false. You may be naturally bubbly or quiet, but people might perceive you as shy. You can't change how others perceive you. Just go with the flow.

Perhaps you are a perfectionist who is always aware of others' mistakes or flaws around them and tries too hard to not make them. Your friend might talk with their hands full of food. This could be annoying. Or maybe your sister laughs too loudly which others find offensive. It's important to learn how to be polite and not laugh too loud while eating. You're just trying to be careful and not do things like that, which could lead you to isolate yourself from people without even realizing.

You have low self-esteem. If you don't like your self or see the value of others, you may have a problem with the mirror. If you don't have to, you may avoid eye contact or even glance at someone. This is a very serious problem. Before you think about it, you must first consider whether your problem is extreme negativity towards others. This problem can quickly spread and can cause more damage than you realize. Sometimes it starts in middle school or highschool, when we try so hard for everyone to like us, that our uniqueness becomes lost under all that "coolness." This problem is still with us as adults if we don't address it.

Is this the right answer? Is it possible? Great! For now, if not, that's okay. Next, accept your shyness. Accept your shyness and acknowledge it. Look in the mirror. You are being honest with yourself. If you are still unable to accept this side of yourself, keep working on it. Continue to repeat these words. You will eventually feel more comfortable around this part. Accepting it can be the first step to overcoming it. If you find it helps, you might say something like: "I've been shy before, and I'm still timid, but not long!"

Now think. What causes your shyness, or discomfort? What makes you feel uncomfortable? Do your family members and relatives gather around and ask you stupid questions about the direction of your career? It could be as simple as a group of friends or family gathering at one place. You might be sharing a taxicab with someone who you are unfamiliar with and have to engage in casual small talk. It could be something new, or you may have to do something new. You know what your symptoms are best. Just before the train of shyness strikes, try to write down the thoughts.

An important side note: It's much easier to resolve the problem when it is just about strangers and not your family. To get to the root of the problem, you will just have to "perceive" these unknown people in the same way that you perceive your friends. They are people or humans with good intentions with their own problems. These people are not your enemies or people who only care about you. When you do this, you'll find that things become much simpler.

Now think situation-specific. Keep track of the conversations and situations you find uncomfortable. With a highlighter, or pen, make a list that makes you feel uncomfortable. Mark the embarrassing situations with dots, and the embarrassing ones with red flags. The list should be as precise as possible. Avoid vague statements like "Family activities." Instead, you can use an example like "When Aunt Marylyn inquires about me about love life." Which types of people make it nervous and uncomfortable? People who have more power than you? What is more important: Money or beauty? This is just for your eyes. Make bold statements, be open and direct, and don't forget to be specific. The more clear you are, it will be easier for you to find solutions to your problems.

This is where the hard part begins.

This will be the next phase.

Start with your easiest case. If Aunt Marylyn happens to be your case, you can walk up to and approach her. Be ready to answer questions about your life and love. You are free to be bold and tell Aunt Marylyn "well, that's personal Aunt Marylyn. And I'd rather not talk about it." You could also make fun of it by saying "Well, I'm not having much luck this week Aunt Marylyn but you will be the first to receive the wedding invite when I get one good." To be comfortable in any situation, prepare for it. Be prepared to face any situation that comes your way. The more comfortable you feel, the less preparation you'll need.

Continue to work through the list in ascending or lower order. Sometimes you may not be able to complete the task on your first try. Perhaps you take a taxi with someone else and have to endure that awkward silence you loathe. Do not despair. Do not lose heart. Just keep trying. It's okay to be a champion.

Chapter 11: Heredity or our Genes

The scientific community has discussed the possibility that our genetic makeup could be a factor in our shyness. Scientists have suggested that some people may inherit a shyness trait.

Generation after generation.

It is not yet possible to prove this, but it would be fascinating if we could learn that shyness may be a genetic and physiological phenomenon. If true, it would amaze if you could find a pill to help you become Don Wan.

However, you can still be serious about it. While shyness is not an inherent trait of personality or genetics, it might be possible to change physiological or genetic aspects.

Here's another example. What happens if someone takes drugs or drinks alcohol? It can have a negative impact on our moods. These chemicals can interact or alter the chemical reactions in our bodies, causing changes in our behavior, moods and actions.

I don't believe that you can overcome shyness with pills or that drinking and using drugs can make you more confident. However, it is possible if you need help. This theory could not only be applied to smoking. It will take some effort to discover the science behind it.

INCONSISTENT PARENTING

Now it is time for you to become a parent. Yes, I'm aware.

For everything, blame mom and daddy. That's not how I'm acting. The truth is that, as I stated in the previous section, the parents are almost always the

The first time a parent has social contact with a child. Parents determine the

The tone of behavior and the mannerisms that are displayed will affect your mental and physical health. When they are loved, children will display their love.

They will show their hatred if they're treated with hatred. They are more self-conscious when they hear it is wrong. This can lead people to become shy or unassailable.

Inconsistency occurs when one parent, usually the mom, has a different parenting approach than the other. The primary parent should be the one who is present for the child every single day. They provide food, clothing, and bathe them. They have the greatest effect on the child.

The father is often secondary parent. He is usually the breadwinner. But not all cases. He works as a family member and makes money by going out. He isn't usually there for the majority of the time. He might be present at night and in the morning. While he may be present on weekends, he may not be available for the child's bedtime. He is frequently referred as the inconsistent parent.

Fathers might not always follow the rules when it comes to parenting. They feel guilty for being absent every day. Sometimes, however, the opposite can be true. Sometimes the father may be stricter or have more stringent rules.

This type of inconsistent parenting can lead confusion or inadequacy among the child's expectations. To avoid this, the child might run from the situation. This behavior will persist throughout their lives, eventually leading to social anxiety.

LACKING PARENTAL INVOLVEMENT

When you are growing up, you need guidance. While I am aware that we are all strong individuals who do not want to accept help or receive advice from others, I believe they need it.

Truth is, we cannot all live on this.

We can't live on our own, so we need guidance from our parents as well as role models.

Two things can occur when parents don't take the time to care for their children's activities. The first is your child will try to get attention. On the other, they might be shy and create their own universe.

Single parents or those who live alone can cause a lack in parenting. The parents or grandparents may work long hours and leave their children to the care of other people. While the parents may not be there, parenting is too challenging. They lock their doors and leave the child alone to take care of him.

You, as a parent must be involved with your child's daily lives. Your child should feel respected and valued by you. Your child should have self-esteem. Encourage your child to be active and go out. It's amazing.

PARENTS WHO ARE PROTECTIVE

On the flip side, parents who are too protective will lead to their children becoming lazy, unsure and unmotivated. If you are excessively protective, you will make your child lazy, unsure or unmotivated.

Tendency to not permit

Children shouldn't be in front of you. If your child is sneezing or having a runny nostril, you should jump. You go to the hospital for your child every time they trip, fall, or trip.

You may think that I am making this up. Parents babysit children, this is what I have seen. My friend kept his son closed off from the outside, and refused to let me accompany him to the mall.

Many television programs show a five-year old breastfeeding in a restaurant. Google would return 1,580,000 results, if you searched overprotective parents. This is an enormous problem with many solutions.

SIGNS TO WATCH OUT FOR IN ORDER TO DETERMINE YOUR OVERPROTECTIVE PARENT.

#

1 GOING TO THE END OF YOUR STUFF

An overprotective parent will typically go through all your stuff and pick out anything they feel you shouldn't have or is harmful. This can range from a blunt object to an entire room.

Take a piece of plastic and make a paperclip. As they

As they grow older, they will start to look for condoms.

#2 SHOW ME ON THE INERNET, OR YOUR PHONE. Parents will use protective software for searching the internet for inappropriate words. They will begin to examine your friends and see "if they've got any", what they are saying about each other. They will look at your phone, internet, and any other technology you have.

#3 BACKSEAT DRIVER: IF THEY DON'T MISS THE CAR, THEY ARE THE BEST

Young adults and teens should drive freely. Some kids see it as a rite. nightmare. GPS and other technology can now also be used to monitor everything by parents, such as your driving speed and break time. You can also use GPS to track your routes. Signs on your car warning you that you are not a competent driver, or worse, that you are "Baby on Board", could make you feel ashamed.

#4 "MY BUBBY IS GETTING ULLIED!"

Parents who are too concerned about their child's safety are more likely be to be worried that they will be bullied at school, or picked on by others.

They must not let their thoughts get in the way. Sometimes, children can become so upset that their parents pick on them.

#5 THEY START TO MAKE PROBLEMS EVEN IF NONE EXISTS

Parents who are too protective can look for problems, even when there are none. Parents will tell their children that they should avoid them or label them as bad influences. If your child does something wrong or is hurt, you will never hear from them. Parents need to allow their children to be children and to have fun.

#6 MAKE DATING AN NIGHTMARE

You will have to deal with your parents if you want to begin dating. You won't want to bring your date with you to meet your parents.

They will make sure you feel like a child in your bathtub.

embarrass your dignity.

Your parents might have a shotgun in front of you at the altar if your date is accepted, or God forbid that you marry.

#7 THEY WON'T TREAT ANYONE LIKE A SEX CRIMINAL.

DELIVERED WITH A GENDA

They will see you if your parents are too protective.

Everyone with a fine teeth comb. They will want everything about them, even before they meet them.

Someone might say the wrong thing.

#8 YOU MUST BE HOME AND IN YOUR BED BY a SPECIFIC TIME

If your parents are too protective

You must always be there. If you don't follow the right route home from school, then you will be punished.

#9 PARENTS WILL USE PUNISHMENTS FOR ANY ACTION THAT THEY SEEM IMPLICIT.

Overprotective parents tend to have an overprotective nature. If you don't fit within the structure or rules they set, they may punish you quickly.

punishments. Some punishments may be stronger

Physical, such spanking or other severe punishments. The majority of punishments are fear-based. Parents can use their control to make the situation more manageable. This can cause a drop in self-esteem as well as social anxiety disorder. This is the most severe kind of shyness.

#10 SPORTS/SOCIAL ACTIVITIES BAD

The last one is social activities and sports. We won't discuss it. If your parent is too protective, they may try to stop you engaging in sports.

Other social activities. Parents will fear for their child's safety and will worry about whether they meet the wrong people or get hurt.

Without social interaction and the skills to deal with such situations, people won't be able.

LACKING EXPERIENCE in SOCIAL SITUATIONS

As I mentioned, people who have overprotective parents tend to have difficulty socializing at parties, gatherings, and other events.

The shy person isn't able to communicate with others on an interpersonal level. A shy person will search for a comfortable environment or a way to appear accepted while still remaining distant.

People who are shy might act out nervously when embarrassed. They may look at their surroundings and move their eyes.

They might also avoid eye contact or rub their fingers together. These children may avoid social activities or be reluctant to make friends. In extreme cases, children may try to isolate themselves.

MODELING BEHAVIOR AND LEARNED BEHAVIOR

As children, our brains pick up on information very quickly. We look at ourselves, our siblings, as well as other people we come across. Two-year-old granddaughter.

She has changed and grown so much every year. I

I was amazed by her actions as well as her disposition. You will need to look within your head to see where she acquired the information.

Children will be more attentive to your actions and words than you are to you. Children will examine every word you say and act. My stepdaughter, however, smokes. My stepdaughter smokes in such a way that it is obvious to her daughter. My granddaughter is now following her smoking patterns.

Shyness can be the same. If they see you shy, their shyness will be imitated and they will become more shy. They will be just like their parents but won't know what that means or how it will effect them in the long-term.

SHYNESS MAY CAUSE PROBLEMS IN SCHOOLS

Shyness is something that most children experience in their childhood. It can be a problem that will affect your life for the rest of it. Most children don't feel shy.

Their first introduction to social interaction will be at school. It is the first taste of social interaction that they will have after going to school.

They are placed in a place with at least 12 to 20,

You may be surrounded by children your age. They will have to follow school rules and regulations.

An introverted student is more likely to get picked on or laughed at in school. Others will consider them strange and force them out of their environment. If a child feels rejected, unaccepted, they will seek to create their own world. This will lead to lower grades, less social growth, and a poor educational experience.

LOW SELF ESTEEM, NEGATIVE POINION OF ONESELF

One side effect to shyness is low self-esteem.

esteem. A shy child will run away from the public and hide. Rejection can be a form of humiliation.

They take it personally.

CHILDREN IN SYDNEY MAY BE VISIBLE TO OTHERS AS STUCK UP

Adults and children can both have high self-esteem. However, it is more common for children to have higher self-esteem than adults. They don't like to be influenced or distracted. Children believe that they are the center, and therefore don't feel any need to be anything else. Children aren't tolerant of others and believe they shouldn't be. If you are shy or do not get along well with your classmates, it could be a sign you are not able communicate well. This could cause you to lose your school experience. It is important to be transparent about who you really are and what beliefs you hold. It doesn't necessarily mean you should do everything. However, it is important you feel confident in who you are.

TOO MUCH CRITICISM, TEASING, AND THREATENING

It isn't difficult to admit that kids can be mean, pick on and judge others just because they differ. It is easy to say this. As children, our tendency is to judge other people based on how they act, speak, and look.

It's simple to put it that way. It will not be something you view as a normal part if you're shy. It will become something you personally experience. You will feel isolated. You will eventually accept your shyness.

THREATENING

Someone who feels threatened will tend to pull back and defend themselves. A person who feels threatened and is shy will tend to curl up in a protective ball, or hide from the situation hoping it will go away. The person who is threatening them feels

Their threat is more powerful because they know who their target is. The threats will continue unabated. Because they are shy, they won't tell anyone.

TESING

Teasing is an alternative to threatening. If you tease someone, they might feel embarrassed or shy. If someone is being teased and they're already shy, it can make them feel even more embarrassed.

CRITICISM

People don't like being told negative things about their self-worth when it is down to criticism. People do not like hearing that they were wronged or that something was better. People will believe their way to be the best. It is unacceptable for anyone in the world to tell them otherwise.

Shy people are more at risk. If someone is shy, and they put themselves out there to attempt something new, and someone criticizes or the results, then the shy person will likely retreat to their world and never try that same thing again.

People who are shy or who aren't outgoing tend to be more inclined than others to read into other people's actions and statements. Before speaking to someone who's shy, you might think about what you can offer.

EFFECTIVE Communication: DIFFICULTIES

Someone who is shy will often be quiet and avoid eye contact. People who are shy tend to gesture with their hands, eyes and other forms or Body language. If you are shy, it is difficult to communicate.

much. You may find it difficult to communicate with others using traditional forms of communication, such as verbal.

DIFFICULTY EXPRESSING MOTIONS

We love laughter, crying, and having a lot of fun. People love to laugh, cry and have a great time.

Come up to your friends and tell them how you feel. The smiles on their faces can tell them if they are happy. The way we talk, walk and make facial expressions will tell you how bad our week has been. Working with someone

It is difficult to determine who is shy. They are not able to communicate their feelings through eye contact and conversation.

If they are having fun at a party, and aren't sure if everyone is there, they might just remain in a corner.

them.

DIFFICULTY MAKING FRIENDSHIPS AND MAINTAINING FRIENDSHIPS People want to be liked and become friends. This is especially important

Social interaction is essential for children because it helps them grow. Depending on your level, you may not be able meet people or make friends. Sometimes it can be difficult to maintain friendships or not get along with your close friends as much. Some people are too shy to venture out with their friends to new places. There might be a location you feel secure in, such your house, their home, or another nearby place. This will make it less likely that other people get into your safety network.

The same events and places your friends go to may bore you. You may not want the company if it isn't there. If you don't make an effort in integrating yourself into their social lives, you might find that your friends are less likely socially to accept you.

DIFFICULTY SELF-CARE

You have a right to speak up for yourself. No one can make you feel inferior or tell you what to think.

to go. Do not be afraid to tell someone you don't love what you do or how it is done.

If you are treated unfairly or in a way you don't like,

You have the right of defence if you are treated in an unacceptable manner

Please speak up

If you are shy and have shy tendencies, you may be more likely to accept and listen to any verbal and/or physical abuse being directed at you. These attacks will continue against you until your shell is broken, you defend yourself or you find someone who steps up and addresses the situation.

Recognize that being shy doesn't make other people behave against you. You should be able react to these situations.

Chapter 12: Meeting New People

Meeting new people, even for someone shy, can be daunting. Why? Because it's the height, of unknownness. It's not like you know them, but they don't either. You also don't understand how to interact with them. Here's a peek at what I do when I meet someone.

"Oh god! What do I say?"

"Did you find my "hello" strange?"

"Why aren't they looking at me like that?"

"Don't just sit there and say nothing.

"Is something on my forehead?"

"No, they're just staring at my face. They're most likely staring at my faces."

"Or maybe, I said something stupid and they're judging you." Better to stop talking.

"But it's awkward if I don't speak."

"What is the best topic to talk about with them?" They are not my friends!"

"The way that they look at my makes me feel really uncomfortable."

"God! I wish there were something else I could do than to stand here feeling stupid with all my hands in their pockets.

"Oh good, they've left. I can actually breathe now.

"Wait...did they leave because we were here? Was I strange?

"Do they really hate me?" It could be because of something that I have said.

"I loathe meeting new people."

Does your inner monologue sound familiar or strange? If it does, it's because it's something that I struggle with for so long. Keep these things in mind when meeting new people.

Relax

Perhaps the most important piece that I can give is to simply relax. It's okay to relax. Although they can seem to be intimidating at times, it is not their fault. A person can appear cruel, but they are really a sweetheart. You shouldn't let fear cloud the reality.

Remind yourself that you are an important person, that no one else is better than yours, that you are not inferior to anyone and that there is no reason to feel this way. Even if you don't even know them. Relax and let the events unfold. You will leave a better impression if you aren't stressed at all.

Be friendly

Being open, friendly and chatty can only be a good thing. People are more attracted to positive people. This makes them more likely be friendly to you. Easy, huh? Even if you're friendly with the person you meet, but they treat your rudely, please remember that it is not your fault. Shy people are so self conscious that they automatically blame their failures in social interactions. However, it takes at most two people to have one. If it does not go smoothly, then you are not automatically at fault. Nine times out 10 being friendly is going to get you points.

Get out there and have a good time.

Don't stand there and talk, I understand that it can be difficult for someone you don't even know to talk to, as they may not know much about your interests. You can't expect them to make an effort if you don't. This will lead to awkward silence, which is not fun for anyone. Do not be afraid to ask questions if it is difficult to think of something to share. These are proven ways to spark conversation.

"Where have you grown up?"

"Does anyone have any siblings?"

"What did college teach you?"

"What do your spare moments allow you to do?"

"What do I do for a living?"

"What music do I listen to?"

"What is the best movie/TV show you have ever seen?"

In general, questions about yourself and your hobbies, likes, dislikes, etc. are welcome. Simply put, people love talking about their own lives and that's an excellent way to get acquainted. You will be able to share something and then you can go on the conversation.

You aren't being judged by anyone

I know. You feel self-conscious. Every new person you meet will be looking at you in a negative light and judging every aspect of you. It's all in the head. I can promise you that not one person will be judging or thinking negatively about you, unless they are the most adorable people on the planet. While they may be asking you questions, you're probably just getting curious glances. This is totally normal and is a way to get to know this person. It's okay to stop worrying about what impression your making and how negative that impression might be. Instead, focus on the conversation.

This is not a real test.

Do not be too concerned about meeting people. This is not a test. This meeting does not determine your life. You will not be graded. Sometimes, you meet someone new and it goes well. Other times, things don't go as planned. It's not so big of a deal and again, it's not your fault. There are going to be some people who don't get along. This is why I offer the following advice: you don't have to be friendly to everyone.

Don't let your first encounter go wrong. It is possible to make amends later. This is what I can tell you - one my closest friends and the person I loved most was someone that I couldn't stand in its beginning. I found this girl to be a bit too sexist for me. However, once we spent more time together we realized how compatible we were and how much our common interests were. We have been best friends now for 10 years. I am trying to convey that you should give people and yourself more than one chance at succeeding.

Meeting new people & dating

This is why I've added it to a separate category. We all know how shy we can be when someone attractive comes along. I am sure you have experienced this, and it is not a lie. The fear of meeting someone you like can make it difficult to be with them. It's totally normal and not something you should be ashamed of. However, it should not stand in the path of love. Let us work together to fix that.

Take pride in your appearance

This is the easiest and most important step. It will help you gain the confidence you need. You can dress up in the best outfit you have, but make sure that your hair is combed and conditioned. A pair of shoes that are comfortable and easy to walk in is essential. Now you are ready for the dating industry to take off! Although it may sound superficial, this isn't a way to deny that looks do matter. When you look great, it makes you feel great. And when you feel great about yourself, it makes you much more confident.

Simply be you

Oscar Wilde, a wise man, once said something like: "Just be yourself; everybody else is taken." It's a valuable and very truthful piece of advice. Why pretend to being someone or something you're not? This will only make things worse. Remember that you are enough. It's worth the effort. The right person won't judge you for your pretenses or wishes. You can also apply my previous advice not to compare yourself to others. Concentrate on your strengths and not your weaknesses.

Have some conversation topics in mind

I'm not suggesting you should memorize any lines. It won't work. Instead, you can take some of that guesswork out by prepping topics for conversation. This is similar in concept to how I talked earlier about meeting people new. Prepare to ask many questions about them, such as about their likes and dislikes. There are two things that will come out of this. Firstly, it will show your interest in them. Secondly, you'll learn more about their lives and get to know them.

Chapter 13: Shake The Shyness - A Practical Guide

This should make you feel like you've made good progress in your struggle to overcome shyness. Although it wasn't an easy journey, you've come to accept yourself as you are. Give yourself a chance to be grateful for your efforts and work.

Implementing more exercises will help you to feel more at ease in situations that you once found embarrassing and introverted. This chapter is designed to be a practical guide. It will cover a range of shyness-shaking techniques proven to improve self-esteem. Take your time, be patient, don't give up, and take small steps back.

1. Visualisation

This is an effective technique that can help those with stage fright, anxiety, and shyness. Positive imagery uses the power of positive imagery, to persuade the brain to see what it is seeing and then act accordingly. To tap into this source, close your eyes and picture yourself in a situation which would make you shy or uncomfortable. Visualize yourself becoming confident, not self conscious and comfortable. Think of different scenarios. Engage with everyone. This will be a great starting point for real-life situations. While it might seem silly to imagine such situations, the brain does not learn from experience. Therefore, this is another brain training exercise.

2.Focus shifting

This technique can prove very useful in social situations for someone who is aware of their shyness. When you notice yourself becoming self-conscious, focus on another person to implement focus shifting. To help them understand, you can use empathy and compassion. Take the time to really feel what they are feeling, and then try to look at things from their perspective. When you can, look for someone who behaves confidently. If you have these traits in your brain, you will feel more secure as you don't have to worry about yourself.

3.Your attitude and your posture

An easy way to overcome shyness and anxiety is to develop a confident attitude. When you act confidently in many situations, your brain will begin to associate these actions and transform them into confidence.

4.Remove the comparisons

Recall that every person is different and the transformation from shyness to confidence and security takes time. Everyone will be at different points and even highly extroverted individuals will have had moments or times in their lives that were similar to yours. Your progress should not be measured by how you compare to others. Accept the fact that you can reach your goal, and that many others have done it. This will make it easier to believe that you are capable.

5.Promote clarity in your speech

The inability to speak clearly in public and out loud is a common issue for shy people. Try practicing in solitude to improve your speech. Then, speak at a relaxed pace while speaking loudly. Try recording your voice with a recording device or a mirror. This will help you to become more comfortable hearing your own voice. Once you've got it down, practice speaking with the people closest to you.

6. Remember your strengths

You are amazing, no matter how many people you surround yourself with. Look at your achievements, your passions, or your skills. Everyone has strengths and weaknesses, but every person also has gifts. It is important to keep these positive traits in your life. This will make you more confident and comfortable in social settings.

There are many roles in each social group. Even though you might not be the loudest person, that doesn't make it less valid. Quieter people tend not to be as attentive and pay more attention to the details. Instead of leading a team, you might be the one people look to for support. Honor your role. It is founded on your personal strengths.

7. Discard the labels.

Stereotypes, labels and stereotypes can rarely be used to accurately represent an individual. You are so much more than the label you put on yourself. Don't be influenced by others' labels. By doing this, you'll stop believing you are any less than your true self. There will be no stopping you from striving to be more. It is not your responsibility to conform or be like someone else.

Chapter 14: Social Anxiety Support

People suffering from acute social anxiety symptoms often act in a way that is not understood. It does not help to treat them differently, or yell at them. A friend or their family is the closest person they have that they expect empathy.

Closed relationships require you to be supportive and patient in order to help them get better. It will take them some time to get there. They will recover faster if you support them and encourage them.

Here are some tips on how to be a great friend for socially anxious people:

Let them understand that you are there to help them.

Take some time to have a talk with them. Engage them in conversation by explaining that you can understand their anxiety.

Socially anxious people are more likely to believe that nobody understands their fears. This causes them to withdraw from all those they come in contact with. This can be avoided by empathizing, understanding and assuring the person that you will be there no matter what.

You can improve your listening skills.

Once socially anxious individuals open up to their feelings, you may find that they share their whole life story. Listen to what they say. This is what they most need: a friend, family member, or acquaintance who will listen to their stories. It doesn't really matter how small-minded their problems are, it matters to them.

Ask them to go see a doctor.

If you see them suffering from extreme social anxiety symptoms, you should suggest that they seek medical attention. However, you should not push them beyond their limits. This could make it more difficult.

You may have to suggest the idea casually to them, perhaps twice or even thrice. Informing them about possible consequences if the suggestion is not accepted. You need to give them enough time so that they are able to discuss the possibility of visiting a psychiatrist for their anxiety disorder.

Do not encourage social anxious behaviors

You should not encourage them to be anxious. If they suddenly decide not to attend a party, don't conceal them. Let them know that if they are going to be leaving, they must inform the hosts. Explain to them that this is a gesture of help. Ask them to defend themselves.

Do not shout or yell at your children

Their behavior pattern has remained consistent over the years. Their behavior pattern is not likely to change overnight. A socially anxious person may take days or even months to make any changes in their behavior. Never shout at or yell to them for falling back into old patterns. Importantly, don't make it too overwhelming. Take each step slowly.

You can handle your own emotions

It's easy to get lost in emotions when you're trying help someone who is socially anxious. However, you should not let this cause you to lose control over your emotions.

Don't be afraid to ask for help

Do not forget to keep your promise to be there for them if they are sick. This can make them feel more down and hurtful. It is important to keep an eye on your loved ones by calling them regularly or having a chat with them over lunch. This will allow you to monitor how their health is doing. Keep them on track by reminding them to take their medication as prescribed and to visit you every so often.

Chapter 15: Acceptance and Commitment Therapy

We will now move on to acceptance and commit therapy. It's an old therapy but is basically a mindfulness form of therapy. It suggests that better well-being includes overcoming negative behavior and decreasing avoidant styles. The next part will address how you commit to change and what you should do if it doesn't work.

It deals with accepting your reactions and being present. Those who obsessively worry about the future or hold on to their past aren't doing well. Acceptance therapy involves accepting the truth of what you have. This means letting go without trying to control them, looking at strengths and weaknesses, and accepting that your difficulties are real. It's the first step that will allow you to see your life for what it is.

The commitment is the easy part. It's about looking at ways to commit, feeling these sensations and looking at what you think of yourself.

Defusion

This is the largest part of defusion. It's what teaches us to accept our thoughts and change our behavior. This does not mean that you should fight the words. You can instead accept the emotions. Also, it means that you need change the difficult thoughts that are holding you back and how you react. ACT cognitively neutralizes these experiences. It allows you to see them as what they are: passing feelings or irrational ideas.

So how does this relate to anxiety? It should be obvious. When you experience social anxiety, you think everyone hates you. Do you think that is a reasonable thought? You are wrong. That you think it is happening to you is a sign that everyone hates you. However, this is not the truth. ACT aims for you to be able see the truth.

This gives you an honest feeling and outlook about your life.

It's amazing what this can do for your life. This new outlook can change the reality of your life and allow you to see clearly what you need to do.

Differences between CBT & ACT

There is a distinction because you are likely looking at it and wondering what the difference is. ACT has two goals. One, to reduce these unpleasant emotions and experiences. Two, to reduce the struggle for control or do away with them. Three, to increase your participation and involvement in meaningful activities.

Simply put: you face your fears and anxieties about controlling them. Instead of succumbing to those feelings, you try to be rational about the experiences. It really does make a difference, and you can take part in more meaningful activities.

Therefore, you aren't running away from the anxiety that comes with social situations or the irrational idea about having to be around certain people. Instead you're better understanding your thoughts, having a better feel on them, and not trying too hard to control these thoughts.

Although they share some similarities, you'll need to use different cognitive techniques that will help you recontextualize what you think, understand different types of narrative, and accept it as the experiences that are right for you. When you are consistent in your actions as well as your personal values, this will become apparent. This will allow you to see the gaps and help you identify the values which can make your life easier. It may be necessary to spend some time on cognitive and values clarify exercises. But they can be a tremendous help with shyness or social anxiety.

To manage social anxiety disorder, you must learn to accept yourself. You'll have greater psychological flexibility, learn to accept yourself and not hide from your negative thoughts. You will gain insight into your thinking patterns and avoidances, as well as the reasons you are not taking action.

This is part 2 of our 30-day program to overcome your social anxiety.

Chapter 16: Managing Unhelpful Thoughts

Shy people have to change their mindset. This is the most significant obstacle they face. Even if shyness can be caused by physical traits that are not desirable, the mental aspect must still be considered.

Positive mentality is the most powerful factor in personal improvement. Many researches have examined the thoughts of shy individuals. It is possible design effective solutions based upon patterns of thought.

Parents of children with shyness problems or adults should remind their children that negative thoughts and feelings are only a product the mind. There is no way to prove that these thoughts are true.

A key step to overcome shyness is managing or dealing with unhelpful thought. These aren't complicated steps. Unhelpful thoughts management is basically about recognizing negative patterns and creating plans to fix them.

Recognizing Unhelpful Thought Patterns

It is often easy to see which thoughts don't work. These beliefs are unrealistic and cannot be supported.

These thoughts can make it difficult for shy people to see the limits.

Almost all negative emotions can be described as unhelpful. You could look at examples and use them as a guide to detecting unhelpful thinking.

These examples can be passed on to your kids by your parents, allowing them to monitor and evaluate your thoughts. Look at the examples below.

a) Before you meet people

"I will be a fool of myself."

"I don't really think I have anything to offer."

"I might blush, embarrass and embarrass myself"

b. In the presence other people

"I am not good at this."

"All of these people are looking at my face."

"I feel awkward. My hands are shaking."

c) After meeting people

"I was an idiot."

"I won't do it again."

"It turned out to be a total disaster. It always is.

Many people struggle to recognize if they have helpful thoughts. It is possible to categorize and outline each thought.

There are a variety of negative thoughts that have been identified. This will make it easier and more efficient to group or identify thoughts. These categories are as follows

Mind reading: You assume that you know what other people think of you. You shouldn't assume other people are thinking about you.

Future prediction: You instantly jump to conclusions regarding the outcomes of events. These predictions are always wrong.

Personal level thinking. The smallest of things is considered to be important.

Naming or Labeling: The names you choose to use for yourself have always had negative connotations.

"What If" thinking: You can be anxious about what might happen. You have to be cautious about the things that are being planned.

Negativity theme

Exaggerated generalizations. Negative generalizations are a constant part of your life.

II. 2. Challenging unhelpful thoughts or ways of thinking

Next is to challenge the thoughts that are not helpful. This can help to solve shyness.

Most times, overcoming negative thoughts would result in positive change right away. But, it is one of many steps to positive change for those with social anxiety.

One must pose serious questions to be able to challenge one's thoughts.

Yes, even young children can do this independently. These questions are broken down into 5 different types. These questions are grouped together with the appropriate examples.

Evidence: Which things are contrary to your generalizations? Ask yourself, what are your generalizations?

These patterns are easy to spot. Ask yourself whether you are thinking negatively without any basis.

Ask your trusted friend for an honest opinion on your current thinking.

Time: Most feelings fade over time. How would you feel about your actions within the next 3-6 months?

Cost of thinking: This helps to determine the potential consequences of an individual's unhelpful thoughts. Ask yourself if you're willing to let these thoughts influence your life.

Alternative thoughts: There are always other ideas that you can create or pursue. Ask yourself if you have any positive (alternative) thoughts that might replace the one your are currently entertained.

It is easy to manage unhelpful thought. Once you have established some of these thoughts, you will be able to set yourself up for success. This will allow you to immediately feel the effects and help you create solutions. You can use one to three challenge questions for a single, unhelpful thought. Look at the example below.

Unhelpful thought: "I won't play in the play." My classmates would laugh at the awkward way I speak.

Possible challenge questions:

"What proofs does my class have to laugh at me?"

"Six Months from now, will my class still care about me awkward performance at the theater?"

"Will my bestie feel happy about the way that I think now?"

"I will join this play. Are my classmates going to be surprised that I can actually perform at plays?

It is possible to incorporate the steps listed above into your daily life in order to manage unhelpful thoughts. This skill can be learned and used by both adults and children.

It is possible to reduce shyness and social anxiety by using unhelpful thoughts management. In the ideal scenario, this is all one would need to get rid shyness.

Chapter 17: Shyness in Business

Shyness is one of the worst things that can happen to your career. A shy businessperson will likely have more difficulty getting a job. You will likely end up watching other people who have joined the company climb the ladder, while you still hold your job. You don't have to be shy in the business world.

We can go back to the image the shy little girl. It was thought that it was a feminine trait to be modest in years past before women entered the business industry. It was thought to be feminine. This is no more the case. To be competitive in the business world, women and men must be both outgoing. A shy little girl can't be successful in the modern world. Or a shy little man.

If you discover that you are shy and fear losing your job, the best thing you can do is address it immediately. You will have your first chance at overcoming shyness in the business world when you interview for a job.

When you interview for a job, you will have the chance to promote yourself to the company. Do not act humble during your job interview. This is your time to shine a light on your accomplishments and extol your talents.

It is possible to overcome shyness by doing a practice interview with a friend. Interviewers are likely to ask questions that will give you a hint about your personality. This type of question will be asked more often if you have attended more interviews. Here are some of the most popular questions you'll be asked at a job interview.

Why would you want to work in this area?

What is your greatest weakness?

Do you struggle to get along?

How do overtime hours affect you?

What makes you feel the most qualified for the job you have been offered?

What do know about this company's operations?

These are all questions that will most likely be asked at a job-interview. Here are some ways to be confident when answering these questions.

Why would you want to work in this area?

To answer this question, you can give flattering information to them about their company and tell how proud you are to be a member of their team. It's not because you want money or that you don't have a place to work. Answering this question should focus on the benefits to them of having you work there and not you.

What do your greatest weaknesses look like?

This question has been asked at almost every job interview I have attended. You would think there are some people who don't know how to answer this question. This is an important question and should always receive a positive reply. This is my favorite answer. Don't answer this question with a negative attitude.

Do you have difficulty getting along with other people?

Another question you need to answer is "no". It's not a good idea to say that you have a difficult time getting along with others or that you lost your job because you had a personality conflict. Even if there was nothing wrong with you, you can be seen in trouble. It is possible that you were working with AtillaThe Hun. But if you spoke out against AtillaThe Hun, you could be considered to be in the wrong.

How do overtime hours affect you?

It is a passion. You will work overtime as much and as often as possible. It would be nice if they could provide a shower and bed for you in your office. If they ask about your job performance, you should be open to hearing their suggestions.

However, there is an exception to the rule. That would be in cases where you are unable or unwilling to work overtime. The employer should be aware that you may not be able to work overtime because you have other jobs or obligations.

What makes you feel the most qualified for the job you have been offered?

This is your chance tell them what you know about their company and how you would benefit from working with them. Remember to be helpful to the company by answering in a way that is beneficial to them. It is important to mention any experience or education you have that will assist you in your job search.

What do know about this company's operations?

Never show up for a job interview with no preparation. Before you meet with the company, learn as much as possible about them. Be positive and not mention the negative. (Was this not the place where the CFO was fired last year for embezzling funds?) When interviewing for a job.

It is easier to be confident in the business world if you understand how to answer job interview questions. Employers are aware that job applicants tend to be nervous during interviews. The less nervous you are, the better your interview skills will be.

There is still much to be done, including how your shyness will impact it.

Most people feel nervous when they start a job. Try to be friendly and open-minded to all people and invite them to lunch. When someone invites to lunch with you, accept. Do not wait for others, ask them to take you out to lunch. This can be a challenging aspect of any first job. However it is possible to overcome shyness by being more outgoing.

If someone declines to join your lunch party, don't be discouraged. You can keep asking until you reach a mutual agreement on a lunch menu. If you are shy, office politics can be a difficult place to be. However, you must navigate them with panache. Start your new job with a friendly, open attitude and be open to suggestions.

It is important to not say anything negative about any person and to refrain from gossip. Respected employees are those who have a good understanding of their work and who avoid gossip and negative influences.

Sometimes, the first day of work you are approached by the "bad egg" in your company. This is common as the old saying "misery hates company" often applies to work. If someone approaches you with nothing but a vested interest in the company, you should be kind and polite. But make sure you're happy with your job.

Be aware of the office politics that can impact your career. The best rule of thumb when working is not to say anything to people you don't want to hear. It is possible to be productive in business if your eyes are open and you don't let your mouth close more than necessary.

Although it is important not to brag about your achievements while working, it is also important that you let the top managers know. They should know when you are working overtime, and if your performance is exceptional. These are the areas where shy people often find themselves in trouble. The shy person might not want to make a big deal about their work accomplishments and may try to hide their modesty. They won't be able to see the good work you're doing if they don't. Let your superiors know what you are doing well to help them remember when they come up with promotions or raises.

Shy people can be disadvantaged when it comes time to ask for raises or promotions. You won't usually be given a raise, promotion, or both. In these cases you will have ask. Even for someone who isn't shy this can be difficult. If you feel entitled for a promotion or raise, you should list your accomplishments and discuss ways you can help the company. The same principle that you do what is best for the company should be applied. A promotion or raise should not be based on the need for more money. You should be prepared to take on more responsibility for more money and a greater position.

An interview is the best way to get a job. Being able to communicate your opinions and make friends in the workplace, as well as ensuring you get paid well for your work, requires someone who isn't shy about speaking up. You can see that it is difficult to be a businessperson who is shy. To improve your business career, overcome your shyness.

Chapter 18: Tips for Overcoming Your Shyness

1. Now, take a deep inhale and let your body relax. It is perfectly normal to feel nervous about speaking with strangers. This book can help you overcome these feelings.

Tip one: When you feel anxious and have insecure thoughts running through your head, stop and ask yourself "hey, self-come back into the moment", instead of focusing on all the unnecessary mumbo jumbo. This tip can be simple. Deep breathing can reduce anxiety. It can also provide more oxygen to your brain which can allow you to think more clearly. This will allow your mind to go back to the present, and you can return to the conversation.

Smile if blushing is a natural emotion. Smiling will disguise blushing and send signals from your brain to make you happy. This can lower your anxiety and help with your anxiety. These are small tricks to disguise your insecurities and get you through the first greeting.

2. Be yourself. Being yourself is essential to being yourself. What do YOU do for work? What do you do when you have free time? What did last night's dinner cost you? What gets you excited? What makes you unhappy? What makes you smile? Would you like to go anywhere in the globe? What are some of your hobbies? What are your hobbies?

You, You, you... you must first get to know yourself so that you can "sell," yourself to others. What are your morals What do you believe in? Which is your favourite sports team? What would be your dream job if you were to win the lottery. Do some soul-searching. Even if you don't know who you are yet, you may be surprised by the results.

3. Acceptance of your self is the key to being who you really are. This is not about self-hate or dwelling on negative aspects about

yourself. Acceptance begins by believing you are going to love your self and working on yourself. Which are your strengths. What are your strengths?

Write them down. For example, "I am considerate" or "I listen well to others." You can then take your notes and stick them around so you're reminded of your strengths on a daily basis.

You can change your perspective and focus on the positive things you have. This will help you to love yourself better. This may lead you to believe that you are not good at anything. I think you are very good at many things. Do you enjoy playing sports? Do you enjoy cooking meals? Are you skilled at painting? Are you good in math? Are you good with video games and math? Do you not know what your strengths are? If so, then try new things!

It's all about trying new things. Find the thing you enjoy and continue practicing until you become a pro at it. Take a lesson in tennis, ride a bike or paint a class. Learn a language. There are so many things out there for you to try, I guarantee you will be able to master at least one of them or hundreds!

4. Self-acceptance can be achieved by letting the past go and allowing yourself to grow. Do not dwell on a past experience that made your shyness or discomfort when you talk to others. Be kind to yourself for blushing and faltering. If you continue dwelling on past experiences, you'll only cause yourself pain or anxiety.

We all make mistakes. Let's learn from our mistakes and create new memories. Take a look at the future. It's impossible to reverse the past, but it's possible to make improvements in the future. These things take practice. It may be difficult to say the right words the first time, but it will become easier as you continue practicing.

5. Changes can be made to make you happy. There might also be physical things you wish to change, like your hair color. Many people find change scary, but you can make the changes you want. It's possible to change your lifestyle to be more loving and healthy. If you feel underappreciated or stuck in a boring job, it is time to go back to school.

When you can identify the things that are making you unhappy, and then take steps to improve your wellbeing, you'll feel more confident. You could start a journal to find out what's holding it back. Begin writing down your feelings each day. You will soon be able visualise what needs to change and can begin to feel happier. You'll get better if you just keep practicing.

6. Believe in yourself, this is easier said than done. How do you fake it until you make your mark? Or fake it to your dog till you get it. Yes, that's right. It may sound ridiculous but it is possible to practice this at home with someone who you trust and in your own

mirror. Make sure you have your shoulders back, spine straightening and your chin high in the mirror. Practice walking in front of a long mirror until it feels natural. Don't be afraid to walk proudly.

Smile and let your happiness shine! Smiling in the mirror at yourself is a great way to show that you are happy in your own shoes. Remind yourself that you are beautiful! Be confident in your abilities, even if they don't come easily at first. The best way to improve your self-confidence is through practice.

7. Another tip is to practice handshakes. The way someone introduces itself and the strength or weakness of their handshake will determine a lot. A weak handshake can make you feel insecure and weak. A hard, overly demanding handshake could give off the impression that you have overcompensated and are in excess.

Also, practice handshakes. Keep your hand firm but not too tight. Your confidence is enhanced by first extending your hands. Ask your friends for feedback and practice the handshake with them. Practice makes perfect, so it is important to practice your handshakes often.

8. Meditation can also help you relax. You can practice it every single day. Meditation has been proven to increase brain function and decrease anxiety. It is a form mind training that uses meditation to increase well-being in all aspects of life.

You can benefit from many articles and techniques that are available online if this appeals to you. Acknowledging your anxiety and stress patterns and making the necessary changes will help you improve your social skills.

9. Your everyday appearance can be transformed to make you feel more confident. Everyday hygiene is important, such as taking a bath, brushing your teeth, and applying deodorant.

It's also a good idea to get a new haircut, trim your hair, and manicure your nails. This will help you boost your self-esteem, as well as your self-confidence. Consider buying a perfume or cologne with pleasant scents, such as jasmine, orange, and lavender. These are calming fragrances that can help ease anxiety and make people feel more comfortable.

10. The importance of dressing the part is not lost. Make sure you are comfortable in your clothes. If you need assistance choosing clothes, they can help. (This is also great conversation practice for you. Ask them their names and get to to know them. Let them know what kind of function you are looking to have. They will be able point you in a direction.

It is important to dress appropriately when you go for a job interview. For men, you will need a nice pressed collar shirt and slacks. For women, a blouse and slacks is a good choice. For a social event, make sure to plan ahead. If you're going to a new restaurant, make sure you know what the dress code is. To avoid stress and anxiety, plan your outfit ahead of time.

11. Sometimes, makeup can cause problems for women. The best part is that you can usually find makeup artists in any mall or makeup store. (They will sell you products and offer advice.

You should let the person behind you know what function you are going to, whether it is a wedding or interview. If you call ahead and make an appointment, they'll do your makeup. When you've learned how to apply makeup, you can practice it at-home in your spare time. Apply it every day and feel how it affects your mood.

12. Now that you feel great inside, let's start the actual conversation.

Tip twelve: Ask questions. If you're open to answering questions and are comfortable talking about yourself, people will love you.

It's easier to think of questions about someone you don't know before they actually meet. Ask about the family, hobbies and occupations of the person you're meeting.

You can also ask your surrounding people questions so you should pay attention to what they are saying. Sometimes awkward silences can be broken by current events or new releases. You can also compliment someone's outfit (so long as it isn't too intrusive) or use the weather.

13. Let's look at how to initiate and approach a conversation. Approach the person confidently, and try to be friendly. Introduce yourself to the person, handshake your hand and ask for their name. Then, start talking about the event.

Example:

You: " Hi, I'm Sandra. Marks is a good friend of mine. What is your full name? "

Then, they might add: " Nice to have you as a guest." I'm Renee."

You might say: "Nice having you as Renee." You could also say, "Isn't that party great? I love all the decorations.

Renee: I love the balloons, paper lanterns and other decorative touches.

You: "

Renee: "I teach at Lake View middleschool."

You: "My niece goes there. This school is great to work for. What grade are your classes? "

Renee said, "Yeah it is a great schools and I love working there because they offer so many wonderful benefits for the children." I teach sixth grade English and Math." It is as simple as that.

14. An occasional awkward silence is inevitable. Do not be afraid to ask questions or share a quick comment. Pay attention to what they are saying and be ready to answer questions.

Conversation starters are great tools for keeping up to date on current events. Make it your priority to regularly read up or watch online current events. You can ask questions like: Have you heard anything about China right this moment? If they respond no, you've got something to talk about. If they reply yes, they will make an exception.

Movies are a popular choice for many people. Even if you don't have the latest hit movie, as long you have seen a trailer, you can still enjoy them. "Have y'all seen the trailer for Quentin Tarantino's new movie? It looks absolutely amazing!

Or you could just comment on how hot it has been. You never know what conversation about hot climate could lead to. It is impossible to predict what sparks someone's interest. However, once they do find it, it will continue to grow. All they need to do is to fish for the right bait.

15. Listen to what they have to say. Trust me, this person wants to get know you. It may

seem scary. What will they think of you? There is no doubt that everyone is unique. We all have our opinions and our morals.

To move forward, you need to take down the walls that have been built up to keep out the negative, hurtful and harmful things that this person, who you don't even know, may say about you. However, if you don't let them in, it will be impossible to form a relationship. The wall is an easy solution, but can leave you feeling isolated and empty. I'm assuming this is why this book was purchased ..... Give them the opportunity to ask any questions you may have. Feeling clammy? Take a deep breath and let it go. Keep smiling even if your cheeks start to blush. They will have seen it all before.

If you truly value their time, they will understand your feelings and have compassion. If you do not cause harm, it is not a good idea to be friends. There are billions on the planet. If it's wrong, it doesn't belong. However if people don't get out there to connect with others, they will never find them. You can have billions of new conversations each day with billions different people, so practice!

16. Tip 16 listen. It's easier to be a great listener than you think. Listen but don't focus on what you want to say next. Listen to what the other person has to say, and then remember what they said. This is when information can be stored for the next time they appear.

Keep in your mind that she loves tennis. She plays in an All-Women's League every Sunday. The next time you see her, you can ask her how your game was on Sunday. We all crave validation. It'd make you feel wonderful if someone remembered your love for mocha coffee from the last time that you met up with them. It's those little things that let people know you are paying attention.

17. Be open to understanding others feelings. People are not all the same. This means that people's thoughts, feelings, opinions, and

ideas may be different. It is easy to learn about people and their quirks by making friends. What may make them mad won't make it mad for you. They might be happy but you might not.

This will allow you to be more open to learning about other people and help you appreciate their uniqueness. Accept them for who and how they are. Or, you can move on from nice interactions with them.

Complement others. People have the same feelings you do. Some people are more comfortable with their own shells and might not get along well at all with others.

18. Finally, surround your self with people that will lift you up. Begin to get to know other people. Then surround yourself with people that will make you feel good. The people who make it easy for you to communicate with them and it doesn't feel like a burden. Find people who will accept you and give you the best in life. Stop hanging

around people who make you feel inferior or depressed.

It's okay to disagree with others in your workplace. Be polite and try your best to make things work. However, it is important to not go out of your ways to please them. Not everybody will like what you have to say and that's okay. You are exactly the person you were created to be.

Chapter 19: Top 10 Fears People Feel

Now that you know what fear is and how it relates it to anxiety, we can discuss the top ten fears people have. Fear can be good. It can even lead to learning. But if you allow fear to hold you back in your relationships, in your career and in achieving your dreams/goals, it can cause you to lose your way. This chapter will identify the top ten fear that are holding people back and what you can do to overcome them.

1) Fear of being disqualified.

Many people shy away from meeting new people and forming new relationships, fearing rejection. Married couples often avoid speaking to each other about things because they are afraid they will be rejected. Do not let your fear of being rejected keep you from speaking to your boss about a raise, or asking someone out on a date.

2) Be afraid to fail.

Fear of failing is one the greatest fears people have. People are more likely to try new things than they are to succeed. It is important to recognize that failure is a part of life. Learning from mistakes can help to make your next move.

3) Fear of being uncertain

People avoid trying something new because they are afraid of being unprepared. Many people wonder, "What is the point of trying something new?" This fear can make it difficult to do things in a different way than they have in the past. It's not a good idea to expect different results if you do everything the same way.

4) Fear of being lonely

Many people are afraid to be alone in a relationship that is not working. Feeling lonely and alone is part of living. It's inevitable. You have to learn to live with these feelings and how to keep yourself busy to manage your fears.

5) Fear of change

The world is constantly changing and evolving at a rapid rate. Many people fear change and thus resist it. It is possible to become stuck or stagnant if you fear change. It can make it difficult to see the amazing opportunities that life has in store for you.

Fear of losing you freedom

Although it's true you should have some fear of losing control, some people let this stop them from living their life. Many people prefer being single, and they are afraid of losing their freedom. Even though you may lose some freedom in a relationship, you should learn to balance independence with dependence to preserve some of your freedoms.

7) Be afraid of people judging.

People who are afraid of being judged will withdraw from social situations and refuse to take on new opportunities that may open up for them. People who fear being judged overestimate their abilities to deal with rejection and how others will view them.

8) Fear of bad situations.

There is one thing that is certain in life: bad events will occur. You have to accept the positive and the negative. People often put restrictions on their lives when they fear the worst. People avoid doing things or going to places because they fear something bad might happen.

9) Fear of getting hurt.

There should be some fear that someone might get hurt. It's not a good idea to be afraid of getting hurt. This is a healthy fear. Some people are so scared of emotional hurt that they avoid being in any relationship. They do not get involved in romantic relationships with others, they keep their family members close to their hearts, and they even avoid friends. They fear that their strength will not allow them to handle the hurt.

Fear of being rejected

Fear of not being good is the last concern. These people fear the responsibility of leading a group. They worry they are not good enough, that they don't have enough knowledge or control enough power. These people often overcompensate by striving to be perfectionists. However, they keep the thought of not being able to measure up to those around them in many cases.

I am a person who has struggled with fear in the past. However, these fears are easily managed with perseverance and hard work.

It's not that I'm totally fearless. I'm just a human being learning that my fears are not the only thing that can stop me from living life to the fullest. I am capable of being smart enough and strong enough. That's enough.

The last two chapters of this chapter will teach you how to conquer your fears, and become more confident. Remember, this is a journey. It isn't going to happen overnight. It's possible that your fears did not magically appear overnight. However, they were a process. This means that it takes time to learn how you can overcome them. Through this, be patient with your self and learn to love you.

Chapter 20: Preparation

Keep your mouth shut about your shyness

Do not let others know about your anxiety, especially if they are competing for a specific social position or recognition.

You should not reveal your weakness or vulnerability to an opponent. While you might not feel shy to most people, being aware of it to friends or acquaintances will help to make you more aware and encourage them to be kind to you.

Simply, reverse the energy. You don't always have to show them your boldness, but you can also tell them about your weaknesses.

Make fun of your shyness

As simple as this sounds, having fun with your shyness or the idea that your shyness is normal will make you more optimistic about your natural personality.

You may be concerned about things going wrong or just want to slow down and get to understand people.

It is important to be lighthearted even when people are talking about your shyness.

People who are familiar with you might discuss your shyness.

Do not be offended Keep your cool and keep striving for improvement.

Your interpretation of shyness can be changed

Uncomfortable does not necessarily mean that you are shy. When you are asked why you are shy, simply tell them that you're not comfortable.

First, identify the reason for your discomfort.

Are the reasons valid second?

Are these risks real?

Or perhaps you feel a little bit out of your control?

It's natural to blush, or even shift your position when someone is bringing something delicate to the table.

Instead of looking at people and trying to figure out if they are watching you, instead observe how others react. Try to focus less on your own thoughts.

Stop Labelling

Stop presenting yourself to the world as the shy person. Do not be embarrassed to say that you are shy.

You don't have the to fit into the brand others label you with.

You are a living creature of change. You can learn with the passage of time.

If people are impressed by your actions, enjoy it! You will become more socially adept as they get more surprised.

You are a unique individual that can grow to be the best version of you. Use the trait you possess to benefit others.

STOP THE SULF-SABOTAGE

As a person, stop criticizing each move. Be aware of when you are thinking about the wrong things.

Practically, no one really thinks of you as much than you do. Let go of worrying about your self and do what you have to.

If you want to think about anything, it is your progress and your positive intentions toward people and things.

Stop putting yourself in a rut. Instead, look at your strengths and be confident. You can find inspirational quotes online and you can put them up on your wall.

Recognize and Honor Your Strengths

Although shyness is an unfortunate trait, it does not make you less of a person.

Relax, think about your strengths, and then sit back. Reflect on the things that you did in the past that were unique and important.

Take a look at the things you excel at and make a list.

This list should be reviewed each morning before you get out the door.

Brag if you need to about your abilities, and the possibility of doing even more than what is possible.

Remind yourself that there are so many things you can offer the world.

Do something for your relationship

People make bad choices and end up in unhappy relationships that don't work out for them.

Don't seek friendships who only remind you about your weaknesses. Be open to friendships that are supportive, compassionate, and responsive to you right now.

Don't be afraid of being vulnerable in your relationships.

Chapter 21: Your Workout Plan To Overcome Fear

When it comes to shyness, medical professionals recognize that there are many underlying causes. This is definitely one way to see it.

Imagine yourself as a painter who is trying to get the perfect gray shade. To darken it, you could either add more white to the mixture or increase its black. To make it lighter, you can reduce the black or add more white. There is more than one way of doing something. The holistic method, when it comes down to the body is best, has been repeatedly proven to be superior.

Thus, it is not just diet that can improve the brain and thus the ability to overcome shyness. It is a combination exercise and diet.

As stated earlier in this book, the objective of the exercise was to give the brain more oxygen. There is another aspect to the exercise. Dopamine, which is a hormone that signals the brain to release when the body is stressed and the muscles work out, can be released by the brain. This is good. The more you exercise the more you feel great. It is a way your body communicates with you about what it wants. When you run, do cardio, or lift iron, dopamine is taken out of three parts of the brain, the substantianigra (ventral Tegmental), and the adrenal medulla.

When we have pleasant experiences, dopamine from ventral-tegmental is sent to the frontal cortical and nucleus. If you are craving brownies, dopamine from your ventral tuberal is sent to the nucleus inaccumbens. You feel satisfied. It's the pleasure receptor for the brain.

Dopamine is responsible for increasing blood flow to your brain and increasing oxygen. The dopamine is also stimulating areas of the brain that are searching for reward. This can give you a feeling euphoric and let you know that all is well. Dopamine is important in enhancing the ability to learn and remember as well as helping to promote healthy emotions. The brain will remember the sensation and desire it again after it has experienced the pleasure.

Clinically, it has been proven that insufficient dopamine or a misfiring dopamine receptor can lead to ADHS, OCD, Parkinson's and Tourette's. This can lead to increased shyness and a loss of confidence. Many find that the best way to overcome shyness, is to get a good pair of running shoes.

Dopamine not only acts as a hormone but also a neurotransmitter. If you have many neurological disorders, you'll be able to get more of it.

To address shyness holistically, we don't recommend that you do your exercise, or even eat brownies. You can get the ball rolling by exercising, and doing it often. This, along with a healthy eating plan like the one from the previous chapter, will take you three-quarters to the finish line.

You need to be aware of a few basic principles in order for the exercise to work. The first principle is that you should do the exercise frequently. It's important to stick with it. Ideal is to get a quick workout in the morning. Every day is a good starting point. For the greatest impact, follow this schedule.

Start slow for 30-minutes, or if your legs are too weak, start slowly with a walk. It is important to keep this going over time. It is crucial that you do it in an open area. Find a park if you are located in a major city. A treadmill is only recommended if it is not possible to do so. It is the last resort.

Once you feel comfortable with this pace, you can go faster and cover a greater distance. No matter what happens, you should keep your pace at 30 minutes. You should not drink water that has been heated or chilled. This way you can keep drinking water throughout the day. Once you are finished, weather permitting, put your shoes on and walk on the grass. This is your "cool down" period. Don't just take a quick shower. You should wait at least 15 to 30 minutes for your breathing to return back to normal.

Once you have done this for 30 day and you have been increasing your distance while still maintaining 30 minutes, add one additional session to your evening run. The first session should be held at daybreak. The second should be at sunset. This should be your daily routine. This is all you have to do to increase your heart beat and get your daily doses.

Chapter 22: Your Mental Exercise Routine

You've got your diet under control, and you've got your easy exercise routine. Now is the time to bring everything together. This chapter will not change your lifestyle, whether you are a working professional or have a 9-5 job. Your mental health is as important as your physical workout.

To get your mental workout going. Start by lying on your back on a cushion, cross-legged. To get comfortable, the first thing is to do this. Before you begin, ensure you have a Do Not Disturb flag hanging on your front door. Next, muffle the phone's ringtone and turn off the radio. No personal distractions are allowed.

Because the term meditation is often misunderstood or convoluted over the years, I won't use it to describe it. Let's just say that meditation is a misunderstood and convoluted word. Instead, let's use a different term: being mindful. You're not trying silence yourself; you're going to connect to everything while sitting silently.

The exercise begins with being mindful of how you breathe. Sit quietly without thinking about time and space. You can just focus on your normal breathing rate. You can listen to your body, feel it and follow it.

Although you may feel differently after the first couple of times, it will not be permanent. After the first few exercises, you'll begin to understand your breadth. Ancient cultures have been paying close attention to the body's ability to breathe. The Christian Bible mentions the breath and the Muslim Koran the same. Both the Hindu Gita (and the Buddhist sutras) all refer to breath. Your breath is the essence of you, and it can be your greatest ally to overcome shyness.

As you get more comfortable with watching your breath, you'll begin to feel calmer and have a sense of peacefulness. You will find this peace liberating as your dive deeper into the next few months. Be encouraged even if you are distracted by thoughts. This just means that your mind functions the way it should. Be patient and let those random thoughts drift by. Don't try to engage with them.

Your breathing is your anchor. Start by counting. Start by counting how long you take to inhale. Then, count the exhale time. Practice your breathing and you'll soon be able see the difference. You'll learn to inhale, exhale, and do it at the same speed.

Once you are at this point, remember to count every breath. Breathe one in, exhale one. Next, inhale and exhale two. Keep watching, continue following and anchoring to your breath.

Once you understand the basics, you'll find it a way strengthens your mind and provides the anchor you need. Once you become comfortable with the technique, you will find that you can return to the breathing exercises for a few moments to refresh your perspective and regain your wits.

Next, take the next step and look at your shyness while you breathe. There is nothing wrong. You do not have to be shy. Just as the reason why you didn't wear your blouse or shirt yesterday does not indicate that you don't like it. It simply means that you want something better. To overcome shyness, it is your prerogative, not your fault. You are not broken.

This breathing exercise is useful too. This exercise can be done anywhere you like, including on the train, ferry, or at your desk during lunch. It will make your mental strength and concentration significantly improve. It works because your mind has become more aware of your thoughts. As a result, you can gradually spread this practice to other areas. You become more aware of each moment and can live in present. When you live in the present, you're not concerned about what the future may bring. To be aware of your breath and live in the moment, focus on it. Nothing else matters.

Chapter 23: How Social Anxiety, Shyness, And Its Effects on Your Life

Although the terms social anxiety or shyness can be used interchangeably, they are very similar. Shyness is the tendency for being withdrawn or anxious when there are interpersonal relationships. This could be used in situations like dating, work parties and other social settings.

Social anxiety, on other hand, refers to the sensation of discomfort and nervousness in social settings regardless of how many people are there. This anxiety revolves around fear about what other people will think of the socially anxious individual. Additionally, socially anxious individuals will become obsessed with being the center of attention.

Here are some reasons why these two issues are related. If you are shy, social anxiety can be a problem. Socially anxious people tend to be introverts. As we have seen, this contributes to shyness. This might sound confusing at first but we'll look at a few examples to get an idea.

Faith, my friend from childhood, has always been shy. Growing up, she was withdrawing from people she didn't know. Her shyness grew as she grew older. She struggles to think of anything to say in a social setting, and she constantly worries about what people think about her. Or perhaps they think I'm stupid?" These thoughts haunt her all the time. It can take her years to become comfortable in a new work environment and begin to interact with others. In the presence of family or close friends she becomes a completely new person. She is confident, funny and very talkative.

Peter is her assistant, and he has never had any problems interacting in social settings. Peter hates being the focal point of attention. He hates the idea that he will have to give a speech in front if anyone asks him. Due to this fear, he turned down several job offers that would require him make presentations to more than one person. He is terrified of public speaking which can hinder his career development and goals.

Marcus, the man that has not been on any date in many years. His friends always tell him he is charming and interesting but he is very uncomfortable when taking an attractive girl with him on a date. His discomfort makes him sweat profusely, struggle with finding the right words, and makes poor first impressions.

All three characters are socially anxious or shy. You can clearly see that the difference is quite thin as you can see from the examples. This is how we can put together the following:

Social anxiety is a problem for some socially outgoing individuals who have to be the center attention in public situations, such as presentations or public speaking. Some people can be uncomfortable in new environments and situations. This can affect their relationships.

Social anxiety is, in short, the fear or concern that one might be embarrassed or humiliated in any social setting, particularly if they are the focus of attention. Conversely, shyness is a person who has trouble interacting with others. One reason to think that socially anxious shy individuals will experience anxiety when they have to be the center of attention in social settings.

As we mentioned earlier, these emotions and feelings can be normal. But if they get outof control, they will have an impact on your lifestyle and overall health. The key problem is distinguishing between the normal rates of each and the not-so normal rates.

To successfully break free from your shyness cocoon, and conquer your social anxiety, it is necessary to first understand their components and the factors that may affect their manifestation.

Parts of social anxiety and shyness

Most people with social anxiety will describe it in the following way: An uncomfortable feeling that is hard to explain or control. Because social anxiety is an emotion, shyness can be broken down into three components. These will help you understand and manage your emotions. You'll also be better equipped to handle social anxiety. These are the following:

-1 Physical part (This refers to the unexplainable feeling).

-2 The cognitive part (This refers to how you "think" or feel),

-3 This is the behavioral part. It's what you do next to the first two.

The physical component

Anxiety in social situations can lead to a variety of physical symptoms. In most cases, other people will see the most alarming symptoms. They could include: blushing, excessive sweating, or other symptoms. Some symptoms can also manifest inwardly. These could include an elevated heart rate or dizziness, nausea and shortness of breathing. Panic attacks occur when the four symptoms of social interaction fear combined are present.

The cognitive portion

This could include thoughts, beliefs predictions, assumptions, interpretations, etc. They all contribute to the creation of fear in the anxious or socially shy person. These beliefs can be different for each person, but you may hear some similar phrases:

- "I'll make a fool of myself if I make that present."

- "I have to be liked every day"

- "Mistakes occur by incompetent folks, so people will think I am incompetent if I make an error."

- "Nothing would make you blush more than to sweat in front of others"

- "Social Anxiety is a Sign of Infertility"

Anybody may harbor these thoughts or be socially anxious. It is possible to become "socially awkward" by imposing such behaviors into their lives. Additionally, when someone is experiencing symptoms such as social anxiety in the physical sense, their cognitive part is at maximum strength. These are triggers. Research has shown that anxiety is not limited to anxious thoughts. An anxious person may also pay more attention and pay more attention information that supports their beliefs than information that challenges them. This is especially true of individuals with higher levels or social anxiety.

The behavioral aspect

Avoidance is a common characteristic of shy people who are socially awkward or shy. A shy person will do anything to avoid social situations. They will flee from situations they fear or those that raise their anxiety. To hide their shyness and physical manifestations of fear, socially anxious and shy people may resort to other methods. They may put on extra makeup to cover their blushing, dimm the lights to hide their awkwardness, etc.

After having looked at the components of shyness (social anxiety), I suggest that you take some extra time to exercise these skills. Break down your anxiety into its various components. This is possible by simply writing down your anxiety and shyness for the three next times you are in a social environment. This is a good idea. Use a journal to answer the following questions.

*What situation is triggering your anxiety?

*What were your physical manifestations of anxiety? Did you sweat, blush, or something else?

*What anxious thoughts did you experience?

*What are the consequences of anxiety?

In addition, I strongly recommend that you use first person as you write in your journal. This is to make sure your questions and answers are pertinent only to you, and not to anyone else.

These three components, anxiety and shyness, are common for anxious people who are socially shy. This is especially true as these three elements interact on different levels. Anxiety, for example, can start as a physical feeling or emotion, such as sweating, blushing and shaking. Shivering, blushing, shaking, etc. Additionally, these physical symptoms could trigger anxious thoughts such "People will assume I am weak" or "People won't like me if I blushed or shake" or other anxious behaviors. These might be vice versa. Anxiety could begin as a thought, then grow into a physical feeling. Anxiety can also start with avoidance.

Medical studies have not identified the cause of shyness or social anxiety. Researchers have identified several factors that increase the risk of social anxiety and shyness. Let's examine some of them.

Chapter 24: Tips to Overcome Shyness

Many forms of shyness can occur at different times in your lives. This can be overcome by increasing awareness and practicing mindfulness. This section of my book will discuss some of the most important ways to eliminate this discomfort.

Learn where that uncomfortable feeling comes from

You need to understand how your shyness manifests in your life. Understanding the circumstances that cause the feeling is also important. It is important that you know what your concerns are during the triggering phase.

Your self-consciousness has to be turned into self awareness

It's important to remember that everyone isn't going to judge you. The majority of people suffer from similar problems such as being too critical. Doing the same thing to yourself will only make matters worse as it can affect your self-esteem.

You need to be uncomfortable in order to get used the situations.

Sometimes it is not your social skills, but your self-confidence, which can make you successful in any endeavors that you pursue. Sometimes, you may be afraid that you won't be successful. The best way to get over fear is to put yourself in uncomfortable situations. The more you attempt to confront the situation, the more you will get used to it. This will help you improve your coping skills.

Identify your strengths

Be confident in your abilities and accept them fully. This can be difficult if your self-confidence is low. Persistence is essential. Your success is guaranteed if your only other enhancing trait is persistence.

Practice your social skills

Your social skills can be improved through practice and experience, just like any other skill. If you're willing to put yourself out there, you will be able to make it through more social situations. If you're having trouble coming up with something to say, practice what you need to.

It is essential to know how to like yourself, no matter what.

Appreciate yourself and appreciate your unique expressions. Writing a letter may be a good way to start this process. You might also write gratitude letters to yourself. If you have time, you could even go on "dates with yourself".

You can be liberated by not conforming and following the rules of society, if done correctly

It can be very exhausting to try and fit in with everyone around, especially if this is a constant effort. You need to accept the fact that you are sometimes allowed to be different. People who are famous have many experiences with insecure, self-consciousness, awkwardness, and insecurities.

You can learn to be more focused on people

Instead of being the focus of all attention in social awkwardness situations, it is better to pay attention to the opinions and experiences of others. Learning about other people should be something you do. You should ask people to tell you more about themselves to achieve this. You can also think about what you really like about someone. This type of approach is not for everyone.

Stop labeling your self

Do not think of yourself as shy. Remember that you are unique and beautiful. You don't have to do anything but leave it at this.

It can have a positive impact on your health as well as your overall well-being.

It is possible to see anxiety and shyness in the form of blocked energy. You can release this energy through physical movement. Walking or jogging are good exercises to re-channel these blocked energies.

Visualization is another way to get rid off shyness

A positive and confident view of yourself can help you see yourself differently when you are actually in it. Next, close your eyes. Then, relax and enjoy a peaceful place. Play some relaxing music and you will be able to imagine your life in the way that it was meant to be. Note how you feel about the scene, the music, the smells and the actions you take. This will make the scene feel as real as it can be.

Relinquish your perfectionism

You may compare yourself to people you know. Even celebrities may lead you to compare yourself with them. If you start comparing yourself to other people, it is possible that your expectations will be unrealistic.

You have to stand up for yourself

There is a lot of potential within words. Your subconscious mind basically "hears," what you tell yourself, and decides whether to believe it or not. Aristotle wrote, "We are all what we do repeatedly." Therefore, success is not an event, but a habit.

That moment should be your focus

You can be mindful of your actions no matter what you are doing. This will help reduce shyness. In order to have a meaningful conversation, it is important that you forget about your appearance and only focus on what you are saying. Allow yourself to be lost in words. Then, take in all that is being said and absorb it. Be aware of nonverbal cues. These include expressions and tones, as well as body language. You'll eventually lose your shyness when you start to appreciate these things.

You must not avoid unpleasant situations.

You are only enhancing your shyness if you try to escape these situations. Instead of running from your situation, it is important to confront it. Turn your fearful situation into an opportunity for personal growth. You must be a watcher while simultaneously looking inwardly.

What is most comfortable?

There are not always people who enjoy going to bars and clubs. That is perfectly okay. It's important to find out what you like and is compatible with. Once you've determined this, you can begin to search for communities and people who will support your potential. You do not have to do what others are doing. You don't have to do the same thing as everyone else.

Learn to accept rejection

You need to be open to the possibility that you will be rejected. It is best to not take action if this happens. You are not alone. Rejection happens at different times in everyone's lives. It's a normal part of life.

Overcoming self-doubt

Self-esteem depends on how much you can trust yourself. You will score high on the self-esteem scale if your belief in yourself, as a person and as someone who is capable of doing things well, and isn't dependent on approval from others, is strong. However, self-esteem can be affected by doubting your abilities and capabilities or not being able to assess how good your job is. You must overcome self-doubt and build self-esteem.

Control self-criticism

We are more likely to be critical of ourselves when we make mistakes. It's a normal way to work towards self-improvement. Do not dwell on the issue or harbor regrets. You may have heard it said that you are your best friend. That's how it works. You're done.

With self-confidence, act

There are ways to overcome shyness. To overcome shyness, you need to feel confident in the face and beyond disappointment. You can reverse your tendency to feel shy and withdrawn when you don't want people to face you. We must tell ourselves that it is nothing big. Don't worry. It's possible to say "I can do it!" and other similar phrases that allow us not to be intimidated or shrink from the task at hand. Even if confidence is not a priority, we can pretend to be confident. This will inspire courage, which can help us seem commanding and in charge, even when we're not so sure.

Connect with others

Shyness is associated with a person who tends not to interact with others. You can make it easier to be involved by talking with people, getting involved in discussions, being part of the discussion, and being part the overall conversation. If we encourage ourselves to take initiative, we will be able to find the ease in joining in and sharing our opinions while also accepting other views.

Know your strengths

Even the most shy person is capable of displaying a wide range of positive qualities. We can tap into these qualities by reminding ourself of who and where we've been as well as what we have achieved. In the rush and excitement of the moment, it is easy to forget who you are and what you have going for. Your "personal selling points" are important. It is a common practice to keep a list of four or five things you are most proud of. You will keep these qualities in mind when you need them.

You can get over the incident

You've done something wrong, you have let someone down or missed an appointment. It happens. No matter how minor, important, or significant the incident, humans are naturally inclined to dwell on it and worry about it. That's fine, it's natural. However, it shouldn't be too much. Recognizing the mistakes we made can help us to be more aware and prevent future ones.

Be kind to people

Who are the people who can make us feel uncomfortable or worse, anxious? Who are the people who gave us trouble? We must not forget the family members we have had bad relationships with. Do not think about these people no matter who they might be.

Be up for the challenge

A defense mechanism for shyness could be described as being a defensive response. This is how shy and insecure people can avoid trouble and stress. The shy person avoids the discomfort of uncertainty and lacks self confidence by standing still. Avoidance is the best strategy when confronted with challenges, making difficult decisions, and dealing with intimidating personalities.

Make the most of your imagination

It is obvious that self-esteem, selfconfidence and other aspects are not physical manifestations of our personality. The same holds true for our imaginations. They are only part of our thoughts. An imaginative mind can have positive or adverse effects on our thoughts and personalities as well as on our physical state.

Practice mindfulness

If you are occupied with other things, thoughts and feelings such as shyness will not be able to enter your mind. Mindfulness or simply being present is the principle behind mindfulness. Mindfulness, which is basically a way to be open to every sensation while preventing thoughts from taking control. Imagine you are sitting in silence, with no distractions, perhaps with your eyes closed.

Motivation and resilience

When the word "resiliency" is used, it refers to something which snaps back into shape after being bent. You can see trees in motion, whipping in strong wind and then bending to the side, but they will quickly return to their vertical position when it subsides. This is classic resilience. Resiliency, or the ability or reflex to recover quickly and fully after any setback or "jolt," is an essential trait in people. Psychologically recovering from a difficult situation and responding appropriately can be vital to personal success.

Conclusion

You have the ability to overcome your shyness. Not being shy has to restrict your ability to have the best experiences and opportunities in life. It can be overcome.

Again, I want to thank you for downloading this ebook. I hope it gave you some practical ideas that you can put into practice in your everyday life. I also hope you have become more accepting and comfortable with your own shyness. You can do it!

Keep in mind to do what feels right. Also, don't be afraid to take risks and follow your own morals and ideals. Not being shy means that you must become more confident and outgoing. You don't have to be shy in social situations. It doesn't mean you need to become more confident.

It's time for you to step out of your comfort zone and try new things.

www.ingramcontent.com/pod-product-compliance
Lightning Source LLC
Chambersburg PA
CBHW050409120526
44590CB00015B/1894